THE OTHER SIDE

"The Only Way Out Is To Die!"

D. R. Meyers

Spirit Bond Publishing

All rights reserved!

The other side restores humanity to the slain woman. She has a name. Her name is Amber Winkenwerder. She has a family. She has friends, Amber was a person, not a statistic. No part of this story may be reproduced in any way. Some names have been omitted. The author has chosen to omit the names rather than change the names. Many nouns have pronouns instead of nouns. This is to protect Amber's family! Amber's story belongs to Amber's family and no one else! Her story shows how the effects of drug addiction and lifestyle change the lives of every member of the family. All rights to this story and everything in this story belong to Amber's immediate family, except her husband! Amber's husband cannot claim any rights to Amber's story because by law they are no longer married. The death he may have been a part of has separated them!

ISBN 978-1-960175-05-2 ©2023 Spirit Bond Publishing: This Copywrite belongs to Amber's immediate family. All rights reserved!
Table Of Contents

Table Of Contents

Forward

Eldest Daughter's Story

Second To The Oldest Daughter's Story

Amber's Only Son's Story

Second Youngest Daughter's Story

Youngest Daughters Story

Daddy's Story

Momma's Story

Chapter One

Chapter Two

Chapter Three

Chapter Four

Chapter Five

Chapter Six

Chapter Seven

Chapter Eight

Chapter Nine

Chapter Ten

Forward

Imagine waking up to every parent's worst nightmare! May 21st, 2021, I had the most unimaginable day. I sat in my partially wore out rocker recliner. My youngest daughter brought my old chair to me several years past. *"It is your favorite color momma. Don't you at least want to see it? It is only seventy-five dollars. Daddy needs a new chair momma."*

Of course, I caved. Amber always had her way with me. Daddy gave her seventy-five dollars, and that old burgundy chair became his rocker recliner. Then we moved and daddy replaced that rocker recliner with a new recliner. That is how that old burgundy rocker recliner became mine.

That morning, I sat in my recliner, gently rocking back and forth. I sipped on my coffee mixed with hazelnut creamer. I began figuring out my day, but something happened. My head got light. I could not focus on anything. My arm went numb. I could barely feel my fingers. My face did not feel like my face. My heart started thumping in odd rhythms. I do not remember putting my coffee down on the table, but I did put it on the table. It felt like I was having a heart attack without the between the shoulders pain. I did not have any pain at all. I sat back in my chair and tried breathing deep to calm myself. It was as if I were dying but it was not me. May 21st. 2021 was the day my youngest daughter died. The weirdness I felt was my daughter's spirit making me feel her departure.

What began as an ordinary day, soon turned into the most unimaginable week of my fifty plus years. I had no idea, until May 27th, 2021, that my youngest daughter had died. May 25th, 2021, my eldest granddaughter messaged me on messenger. She wanted to know if her mother had contacted me. I was returning her message when my dryer began beeping, morse code style. I do not know morse code, but the beeps were deliberate, and I could feel my daughter. She tried to let me know that something horrible had happened. The morning of May 27th, 2021, Ambers eldest daughter messaged me, and almost at the same time, Amber's only son messaged me as well. My grandchildren wanted my phone number and address, but they had my phone number. Around 5 PM on the 27th of May, two cars pulled up in front of my home. I was not surprised when I saw the sheriff's symbol on the side of the car. A plain car pulled up behind the sheriff's car. I knew why they were there. I leaned against the inside of the door and waited for them to move towards the house. Their faces were somber. The sheriff positioned his hat on his head. His face was full of purpose. I can only imagine what went on in his head. It must be terrible to have to gather your senses and walk up to a total stranger's home to give them such news. I braced myself as well as I could. I opened the door ready for their news.

Mrs. Staff? Yes, what can I do for you two? *Well, Mrs. Staff, we are here because your eldest granddaughter sent us with news of your daughter's death. We do not know the details. You will need to phone your granddaughter for the details.* He handed me his card with the number I needed to phone written across the top. *We are only here in an official aspect.* I walked across the porch to sit down. The official news affected me more than I had expected. Somehow, I managed to hold myself together. I wanted to yell I am fine, go away, at the two official men standing on my porch. Instead, I tried to excuse myself from their presence. I needed the safety of the inside of my house. They kept asking me if I was sure I was all right.

I kept repeating that I would be all right. My husband should be on his way home from work. I would be fine. I just wanted to go inside and call my granddaughter. They left as somber as they came. Heads down to their prospective cars. I watched them pull away from the curb, then I dialed the number on the card. My granddaughter's familiar voice answered my call.

This is my youngest daughter's story. This is our family's tragic legacy. This story portrays Amber Ann Decks life in a more humane way than the news articles you can find all over the internet. I am Amber's mother. I authored this book. I paid for Amber's autopsy. That autopsy told me how my daughter had been tortured before being shot twice in her chest. The autopsy was not mentioned during either of Amber's trials. Amber's case never went to trial. Amber Ann Deck was a mother of five. Amber was a sister to four. She was my baby girl. This answers the how, the why, and the what happened. This is the story every family needs to read. Read it for closure. Read it for answers. Read it as reference. Just read this story.

Now days, many families find themselves caring for their loved one's children. Covid is not a pandemic. Drugs are. There are not enough services for families affected by drug addiction. There are so many excuses. When you need the system to protect your family, you and your family will be let down. Number one rule; the system, including victim services is not your friend. They were put into place to protect the government, not the victims. Victim services is a fancy name put into place so the government can say they offered victims' families valuable resources such as an advocate who protects the family of those who have been affected by traumatic events. Events like murder! Protection for victims' families does not exist! Amber's children begin this book with how they felt about the life and death of their beloved mother. Anyone that suffers with addiction of any sort needs to read this book. That is why our family tells our story. If our family can help even one family, our story mattered. Amber mattered. She would want her story told to help others save their loved ones from the pain she knew she could not save us from.

ELDEST DAUGHTER'S STORY

Amber's Eldest daughter was born late April, in the Norfolk, Norwich hospital in the United Kingdom. Her parents are Amber, and Lance Deck. Her grandparents are Carol and Trevor of Harleston, England, and Ladonna and Dino, and Donald, all from North Platte, Nebraska. At the time of her birth, her father lived in North Platte, Nebraska. Her parents married on February 14th. Amber was pregnant with her second daughter when they married.

Shortly after their marriage Amber returned to America with Lance. The couple began their life together in North Platte, Nebraska. Did I want them to be together? No, I did not! I made it no secret that I did not like Lance. He was abusive to Amber. Lance knew Amber was not 18 as she claimed she was. Yes, she lied about her age, but he preyed on her youth. Lance could have walked away, but he did not. Lance adored his first daughter. She meant everything to him.

There is something about your first child. Amber's first child spent the most time with her. In the beginning, before the drugs set in, Amber and her eldest daughter were the best of friends. They went everywhere together, and did everything together. When Amber and Lance separated, they shared custody of their first child.

Lance died Dec. 18, 2010 at the age of 33. Coincidently Amber died at 33 as well.

Amber and Lance had an understanding with each other after they divorced. They would not let their dislike of each other effect their daughter. Amber vowed to never keep her eldest from her daddy. After Lance died, things changed. Her eldest daughter lost her protector. Lance was very protective of that daughter. After her father's death, Amber's eldest spent the most time with her.

AMBER'S ELDEST DAUGHTER'S STORY

I didn't' realize my mom was an addict till I was about 8 years old. She was pretty normal for the most part or so I thought. It wasn't till I was older that I realized nothing about our life was normal. I love my mom more than anything and I do not blame her for anything. Yes, her decisions were her choice but her mind was not in the right place and I blame myself for the fact I did not help her. Instead, I did blame her because I did not know how addiction truly worked.

I've learned a lot since my mom passed away. I wish I learned this all when I had the chance. I did try to help my mom many times and many times I did. Maybe not in the ways I would've liked to but I did my best as only a kid would know how to.

It wasn't until two years before my mom died that she really started to get bad. I moved to Colorado in 2019 to live with my aunt. I was 15 years old, it ended up not working with my aunt and I wanted to leave very badly so I called my mom to come get me. My mom was in California at the time, she had been there and Oregon for about 4 years. She left Nebraska because she had turned in some bad people in the town, I grew up in.

They were very dangerous so she had to leave for her safety until things calmed down.

My mom was involved with the cartel in the town I grew up in. Those are some of the people she turned in. She did not want to be involved but the minute she went in she couldn't leave; it was too late. So, she wanted to help bring as many of them down as possible in which she did. Back to where I was before, my mom came to Colorado but it wasn't long before she wanted to leave. I think my mom caused a fight so she had a reason to leave.

We were about to go to sleep my mom was on the futon I was making a bed on the floor we were talking and my aunts cat jumped up onto my mom she clawed my mom when she did that and my mom got mad and threw the cat off of her. My aunt was in the kitchen and heard my mom cuss at the cat and asked what happened. My mom said the cat scratched her and said F*** that cat. My aunt got mad so then my mom got mad and they started arguing. It got pretty ugly so my mom said she was done and we were going to leave the next night. We were there for two days before we left.

My aunt was going to sell her Durango to my mom but my mom needed to pay for it. My mom decided not to do that and just take the car when she decided to leave. I told her we shouldn't and she said we had no other choice that we couldn't stay there. I knew there was something else she could've done but I didn't argue with her she taught us not to question her, argue with her, or go against what she told us to say or do under any circumstance. She made that very clear so I rarely did, when I did the consequences were not very fun.

So, that night we left. We waited for my aunt to go to sleep and at about 12 am we left mom wanted to go back to California. We got to Florence which is about 15 minutes away from canon we stopped to get gas and a cop pulled up and turned on his lights. My mom said "fuck" under her breath. The officer got out of the car and walked up to us.

He said "ma'am are you aware this vehicle is stolen?" My mom said "no it isn't. My sister is selling it to me" the officer said "well, your sister says otherwise. She says that she is selling it to you but you haven't paid a dime so it isn't yours yet and you left taking the car. So, you're going to have to take it back, then you're going to have to come with me."

My mom then said "you can take the car back but please don't take me to jail my daughter has no one. I don't want her staying with my sister anymore I was just trying to get out of there because my sisters crazy". He said "okay, here's what we're going to do. I'm going to take the car back and I'll get you guys a hotel room here in Florence while you figure something out."

We went to the hotel there and he got us a room for three days. She ended up deciding I was going to go back to Nebraska and live with my friend. She was going back to California so she said that we needed to go back to my aunts so my mom could ask to use her car again. She agreed and we met my uncle in Colorado Springs he took me back Nebraska.

My mom was supposed to come back with the car and give it to my aunt.

Mom was supposed to get a ticket back to California but that did not end up happening. She had stolen some people's identities along with their money and went to cripple creek. She gambled up there and I suppose she went to try and get more money by gambling to get a ticket back. But she had smoked some weed while she was driving and the surveillance at the casinos saw her. She got pulled over. Well, she had also been called in because she was not back in time to bring the car back. My aunt assumed my mom had taken the car again.

They searched the car and found the stolen items so she was arrested. I was made to go back to Colorado with my aunt while my mom was in prison for a year and a half. In that time, I visited my mom here and there until she got out. But when she got out, she was sent to the halfway house in pueblo.

That is when things started going downhill. She had told me that it was horrible in that halfway house. The staff didn't care about the people there. People overdosing. People going through withdrawals and crapping in buckets or trashcans because they couldn't make it to the bathroom in time. She wouldn't be able to leave yet.

The conditions at the halfway house made mom want to get

out the fast and easy way. She chose that way most of the time anyway. When she did get to leave the very first thing, she went to do was find drugs to sell to get money to get out of the halfway house. She did find a way out of the halfway house and she met a man.

She told me about this guy.

She seemed head over heels about him but he lived in the men's part of the halfway house. I didn't like the idea of her dating yet another drug addict when she was supposed to be getting clean and doing better to get out of there. It didn't last long with this guy. After 3 months of her being there she was finally allowed to leave because she had found an address. My mom met a lovely elderly couple at a church she started going to they offered to let us stay with them till we got on our feet.

With that being said my aunt took me to my mom and we went to the peoples house we were going to stay at. She introduced me to them and we went to the room in the back they were letting us stay in. It took less than two days before we were out of there. My mom had told me that she had to go make $4,000 back because the guy she had been dating that she met in the halfway had stolen the drugs my mom was selling.

She was gone pretty much the whole day the first day. Same with the second but she was there the second day up until 12 o clock. Then she left for a bit came back at about 3. She chilled with me for about 30 minutes before she said she was going to take the dog on a walk. I asked if I could go, she said no she was just going around the block.

I was concerned at first but then I thought well, she's just taking the dog on a walk. Well, 6:00 p.m. hits and she was still not back. So, I start calling her phone she doesn't answer the first few times and on about the 7th call she answered. She sounded flustered. My mom said "I will be there soon just hang on Lexi I'm fine" and she hung up.

While I called, I ran outside to see if I could see her anywhere I did not and the dog was still in the backyard. I went back into the room and 15 minutes later the cops show up and I get told to come into the living room.

The cops start asking me when's the last time I seen my mom and questions like that. I said "she was just here but she's been gone for an hour and a half and she was supposed to have taken the dog on a walk but she never came back."

The old man said "that's a lie her mother hasn't been here all day yesterday and all day today. She comes for a couple minutes then leaves again. I don't feel comfortable having a young lady in my house alone without her mother here." In which I understood. The cop said "well if your mother isn't here you can't stay here by yourself" I then said "please just wait my mom's coming soon I just got off the phone with her."

We waited 15 minutes. My mom showed up in a gold Cadillac. She talked to the cops. They left and we got our stuff together. My mom thanked the couple for letting us stay with them and we left with the man in the Cadillac. I never met him before. My mom introduced me to him and said we were going to stay somewhere else. She then started telling me what happened.

She said "remember how I owed money for the drugs that got stolen by that guy?" I said "yes?" she said "well this man here is a debt collector. He came to collect the money I owed. I did take the dog on a walk but as I was walking by the gas station, he pulled up on me and told me to get in the car so I did and we brought the dog back.

He said I can either work for the money or die He held a gun up to my head. This dude thinks I'm weak but I showed him. I looked at that gun laughed and looked out the window" she said the guy started laughing.

I was so confused because first off why is my mom so calm right now when she just had a gun to her head? And why were we going with this guy? He didn't say anything except his name. We pulled up to this big white house and we got out. I did not have a good feeling about this guy or the situation we were now in. We went inside and I was introduced to a lady. There were kids toys and clothes all over and the lady seemed like a normal lady.

The whole situation was very weird because that lady was who my mom owed money to. It was crazy to think that a normal life like this lady had had a hidden secret. She ended up figuring out the money issue while I went and stayed with my boyfriend at the time. She came and picked me back up when things were settled but when she came and picked me back up, she was still with the man who had the gold Cadillac. I knew what this meant. She was now seeing this man who had just held a gun to her head a week before.

I stayed silent as we were driving and I think they noticed I was upset so they decided a way to cheer me up was for me to shoot a gun. Mind you I have never shot a gun before that besides a BB gun. I was hesitant at first but then I thought maybe it would make me feel better so I shot it out of the window on the highway I got so scared I almost dropped the gun. We entered pueblo and went to this other man's house who was apparently the other man's uncle.

We lived there for a while until we ended up getting raided by the FEDS. That day was pretty crazy I must say, my mom wasn't even home when all of that happened.

We got raided because my mom's boyfriend had gotten busted for selling drugs, guns, and he was a suspect in a shooting on the highway. Our lives had completely changed after we moved to pueblo. My mom did things she never did in her life. That is when she started using more than she ever had before.

She eventually seemed like she was alive but the light in her burnt out. During the raid my mom had managed to get away. The police had found my mom and her boyfriend at the eye doctor where his cousin had an eye doctor's appointment. They got my mom's boyfriend but my mom managed to escape out the back door.

She told me during the raid at our house she was only a couple of blocks away watching what was going on. I was glad she didn't get arrested but I was mad at the same time this was all going on. I never experienced things like this before. I went to my grandma's or a friend when things got bad with my mom before.

Since we were living in Colorado, I had no one but her. So, my mom's boyfriend got arrested and I went to my mom's boyfriend's mom's house. My mom showed up the next day and my mom asked my mom's boyfriends mom if she can help get us a place till my mom's boyfriend got out. we found an apartment and were put into that.

A month later my mom had my siblings come to live with us. We all lived together in a one-bedroom apartment.

Things are alright there for a while but then my mom starts getting into the same stuff again and she starts having people come over. They were not very good people and were on drugs. Which I don't judge those who do drugs. I just do not want that around our home, me or my siblings.

Before my siblings had come and we had gotten that apartment my mom and I had found a trailer out in the county which is a part of pueblo. My mom was very stressed out due to what was happening and things were going downhill more and more and she was also getting high so we fought a lot.

One day we were fighting and she punched me in the face. I went flying into the wall. She hit me so hard my braces got stuck in my lip. My mom never hit me before in my life nor my siblings so I was shocked that she did that and she was honestly quite shocked herself, but she was so angry and stressed out. She did not apologize till hours later. I'm not here to talk down on my mom or make her out to be a monster. I love my mom more than anything and I am not mad at her at all.

I speak of these things to show how much the drugs and problems that life created ruined my mom. She no longer even recognized herself. That moment she hit me is when I knew things were truly not okay and may never be again. I still held a small piece of hope that one day things might be okay. So, when my siblings came things were good for a while. It was summertime so we were mainly at the pool every day.

My mom found a job working for my mom's boyfriend's mom cleaning her house and running errands for her but then as I said things took a turn for the worst.

My mom had people coming over and they were not doing good things when my mom was not around. She was rarely around during the time we lived in the apartments I took care of my siblings from the minute they woke up till the minute they went to sleep. I stayed up waiting for my mom to come home.

Sometimes she came home. Most of the time she wouldn't. When she did find her way home, she showered changed into clean clothes and left again in the middle of the night. Our mom dropped by to give us money for the pool or something to eat. Sometimes she gave us a ride to the pool, but she never stayed longer than a couple hours out of any day.

I eventually got tired of taking care of my siblings all day every day. So, I asked my mom to start taking care of her kids again because they were not my responsibility. Asking her to take care of her kids created a huge fight. My friends were at our place at the time. That is why I brought up the topic.

I wanted to go hangout with my friends. She slapped me in front of my friends and my siblings. That was the first time my siblings ever saw me get hit. They were so scared. My friends left after my mom kicked them out. My mom and I were alone once again with my siblings. I know it sounds like I'm bashing my mom, but during this time there was really nothing good going on.

One day while we were at the pool, I received a call from my mom. She told me not to go home for a couple hours. She had been arrested on a warrant she obtained due to the charges her boyfriend faced during the raid a while back. Someone had tipped the police department of where we lived. It was a lady my mom stole from apparently. That's what my mom told me. So, we went back to the apartment but all the doors were locked and we didn't have a key so I called my mom's boyfriends mom and she came and picked us up at the taco bell down the street.

My siblings were so sad. They had been let down once again and at that point I was completely used to it. I just knew what I needed to do. So we go to moms boyfriends moms house we stay there for a bit and then my grandma comes to get my siblings and I. As we were staying with my mom's boyfriend's mom all they did was talk about how they knew what my mom was doing.

They claimed she was doing prostitution they constantly tried to get me and my siblings to believe my mom was doing horrible things. We would not believe that certain thing about our mom we know she did make bad choices but we knew our mom would never do something like that they claimed they had video surveillance of all of this which is not possibly true because they would not show me the proof.

When we went back to my grandmas, I decided to come back to Colorado to live with my friend in canon city that ended up not working out so I ended up back at my mom's boyfriend's mom house she disliked me even more when I came back but she chose to take me in by her sons wishes. I then became her maid and errand runner as my mom had been for her, I realized how horrible they treated my mom when I took on the role. No matter what we did it was not good enough but she wanted us to do everything for her despite it never being good enough in her eyes. I soon got kicked out and moved in with my boyfriend at the time. As soon as my mom got out, we got a hotel room and I moved out of my boyfriend's house.

Eventually my mom's boyfriend got out and we got another house things started to be really good the best they've been in a long time both my mom and her boyfriend were sober when they got out and continued to stay sober for months then it came to our attention the case had been opened back up with the shooting on the highway that they had served time for so they decided to marry in order not to testify against each other it was not out of love it to save my mom's boyfriend from being charged and my mom would've kept quiet and not have "snitched" on him so in order to save each other both the trouble they married.

The whole thing was a sham the day they got married they were both mad at each other and fighting yet in the pictures they looked so happy. I wasn't even there nor were my siblings. I did not decide to go because my mom had thought me and her fiancé were sneaking around behind her back because he opened the door for me before he did her when we got in the car so chose not to go because I did not even want any of this to begin with. I put up with it all for my mom's happiness but I saw that she wasn't even happy and clearly didn't trust this guy if she could make such an assumption. My siblings didn't even know the man she was marrying the whole time they were in Colorado he was in prison and they had only been together for about a year.

I was the only one in the family who had met him. My siblings came to live with us a month after my mom and her now husband was married and everything was good for the most part. We were having family outings we spent a lot of time together laughed together we celebrated my brother's birthday by riding four wheelers my mom was so happy that day to see us all together and having a good time. I was truly happy myself to see everyone happy. It wasn't until my mom's husbands' nieces quinceañera was coming up that everything started to go wrong yet again.

My mom and her husband were setting up in a different town for the party so they weren't home much and I was taking care of my sibbing's there was a situation where one night where we were watching movies down in my mom's room and we heard the doorknob to our backdoor being rattled the doors and windows were all locked thankfully but someone was at our house for about an hour someone or a couple people it sounded like were rattling the door knobs banging on the door but no one would answer my boyfriend was living with us. He had thrown stuff on the stairs in case anyone came in they would trip down the stairs as soon as they walked in my siblings were so scared.

My mom and her husband didn't come home until the next day in the afternoon and we had found out the people were at our house to scare us because they knew my mom and her husband were not home.

I did not know who these people were as I did not see them but my mom was very concerned. Her husband on the other hand was acting like we were overreacting. The quinceañera comes and my family go to it. I decide not to go. They come home the next morning and everyone's in horrible moods and my mom's all bruised and cut up I asked what happened and my mom said that we were getting kicked out and I need to pack my stuff. I was so confused.

My mom then told me that a situation happened at the party. One of the little boys at the party tricked my brother into biting into a balloon filled with hand sanitizer. The other boys were having a challenge with water balloons who could drink the water balloons the fastest. So, my brother joined in and they filled one with hand sanitizer for him. He bit into it and freaked out because he couldn't breathe and his throat burned, he ran into the house to find my mom.

She was laying down with a headache and she started freaking out because my brother was and he then told her what happened. A mother would make someone snap so she went into the garage where everyone was at and started yelling at everyone demanding answers instantly.

Everyone started yelling at her and getting in her face she saw the mother of the kid who gave my brother the balloon and started yelling at her. Well, she was pregnant so everyone started freaking out on my mom. My moms' mother in laws sister punched my mom in the face. My mom's husband's sister tried to fight my mom they all were ganging up on her.

My mom's mother-in-law was laying down as she also had a headache. She came out to see what was going on and my mom was furious she told her mother-in-law "Fuck you and your whole family I'm done with you guys" and my mom's mother-in-law said "fine well get the fuck out of that house that we rented to you then since its fuck me". So, we moved out and found another place on the east side of pueblo and that is when things truly took a turn for the worst.

All the money my mom and her husband had saved up went into the new house we rented it was in horrible condition so they were out even more money to fix the house up. While my mom and her husband were in the other town setting up for the quinceañera that is not all they had done. They both started getting high on meth again my mom's husband confessed to me after my mom's passing that they had started getting high when they were setting up for the quinceañera.

A part of me knew it because when my mom got high that's when things got bad, she would lose herself, her jobs, our houses, our cars so when we started losing everything so quickly yet again after the quinceañera I knew it had to be that. They started getting higher when we moved to the new house.

They started constantly fighting with each other. Me and my siblings started fighting each other. It was nothing but chaos. Our bills started being unpaid we started having little to no food in the house my mom's husband stopped working and my mom could not get a job due to her having a warrant for something. I do not remember.

They both stopped coming around and when they were around it was nothing but arguing. My mom was in a permanent bad mood once again. Her dreams were crushed and her hopefulness was gone. She then claimed that she had cancer. Yes, I was as surprised as you may be upon reading this. It came out of nowhere and she said it was stage 3 thyroid cancer. Shortly after she started "chemo therapy" every Monday she had an appointment and she would not allow us to know anything else or go to her appointments.

She started losing her hair and throwing up all day and would stay in bed. It was weird because her autopsy showed no signs of any cancer or any tumors of any sort or any chemo radiation effects. My mom started to get better and then she was right back to leaving again. It was as if she didn't want to be around. My mom and her husband started fighting even more. Those fights started to get physical and she then started being physical with me again.

I think in her mind she saw me as an adult because I was older. I started to stand up for me and my siblings more. She and her husband had also started to get physical with my siblings. They were never around but when they were all they did was get onto my siblings. They started spanking my siblings with belts and that is something my mom had never done or allowed any of the men in our life to do.

I learned why they were both so angry all the time. First, they were getting high all day every day. At that point and they were having issues outside of our home with people my mom's husband was in prison with.

One of my mom's husbands' enemies got out of prison and first thing he did was come look for my mom's husband. Well, he found them eventually and one night they shot at my mom and her husband while they were out at the gas station. My mom's husbands' sons happened to be there visiting for Christmas break they lived in New Mexico with their mother and had not seen their father in 7 years. That was their first time meeting us as well.

Well as that all went down that night my mom called me to get my siblings and get out of the house because the people were coming there next. We had no car so I had to have my brother ride his bike to my mom's husbands' brothers house down the street. I did not want him to but we had no other choice he then came back and my mom's brother-in-law came in tow after him. My siblings got in the car I stayed behind so my dogs were okay I wasn't going to leave them behind. I took my dogs across the street and waited in the dark to see if anyone was coming.

A car pulled up and 4 people got out. They kicked down our door and were in our house for about 10 minutes before leaving. I waited around 20 minutes before I went back inside. When I went inside the house everything in the kitchen and living room were broken.

Our rooms were all busted into and our stuff was thrown about. Nothing was taken. It was all just child's play. Angry criminals trying to scare each other like little boys but instead brought guns and fear into our life. It is not fun and games to mess with a family especially children! We stayed in a hotel for a couple nights and my stepdads' sons went to their grandma's house.

After that all happened and the fighting between my mom and her husband his sons did not want to be around their dad anymore and refused to come back to our house.

We happened to get pretty close with them and they loved my mom a lot especially my stepdads' youngest son. They were heartbroken when they learned my mom had died. But after the shooting happened, we went back home after a couple days and cleaned up. A month later our bills are no longer being paid my mom and her husband were gone even more now covid was at its highlight so schools were shut down and we were doing online school.

My siblings refused to do their work and my mom refused to do anything about it. I tried to help my siblings do their online schooling. I got hit for it or threatened to get kicked out. I eventually stopped caring and would stay in my room all day. The house became messy the fighting became more abundant and eventually my mom got tired of it and stayed gone unless we weren't there. We were all very stressed out with everything that had happened.

I picked a fight with a mom one day asking her to start taking care of her children. Again, it was not my responsibility. I could no longer keep doing this. So, she got very angry kicked my door down I begged her to get out and that I was sorry and wouldn't say that again but she snapped. She kicked me in the stomach started punching me in the face saying "I fucking hate you!! I hope you fucking die. "You stupid little bitch" and stood on my chest until I could no longer breathe.

I found the strength to push her off of me. I got into the corner of my bed and screamed "GET OUT!!!" She ran to my sibling's room and I thought she was going to hurt them too. I thought she finally snapped and she was going to kill us all. So, I ran out of the front door around the block to some random persons house and I banged on the door and begged them to let me inside. An older man in his 60s I believe answered the door he asked me what was wrong I said please let me in I don't have time to explain. He let me in I said I need to use your phone to call the police he said why and I just broke down crying.

I said my mom's gone crazy she's trying to kill us I need to call the cops I left my siblings there I don't know if they're okay. I called the cops and they said they'd be over shortly I thanked the man for letting me use his phone and I left back home to meet the cops but when I got there, they were already there and my mom was talking to them she seemed perfectly fine now and my siblings were standing next to her hugging her.

The cops walked up to me and asked what was going on I told them my mom's trying to hurt us. I told her I didn't want to take care of my sibling's anymore that it was her job and she snaped. They laughed at me and said Well what do you expect? You're supposed to do what your mom says no matter what.

I said "that is not true at all. I get I have to listen to my mom. I do. I have been and I'm tired of taking care of kids that aren't mine. The cops then said Well as an older sibling it is your job to help with the kids. I just gave up because they were not going to listen. And then they said my mom said I was the one acting crazy.

She said that I started hitting her and cussing at her because I didn't want to listen to her and my siblings were young and scared so they agreed with her and lied to the cops and again we were taught to lie for her. They didn't know any better. I genuinely thought I was insane that I was the problem. I thought that I was making everything bad because every time I did try to help or fix things, I got hit for it or told I was the problem.

I decided to leave that day after all of that. She told me "If you leave do not think about coming back here again" I honestly didn't want to. I had my friends pick me up and I went and stayed with them in Cotopaxi Colorado. I left in February and it did not take long for things to fall apart while I was gone. My mom's husband got arrested due to an assault charge. A while back when we were living at the house, we had that was owned by my mom's mother-in-law we had some neighbors across the street that we befriended.

There were 4 girls one of the girls was 14 and a drug addict. How she got into that I do not know but she had a guy who was in his late 40s early 50s come and bring her drugs in exchange for sexual favors. That is not the only girl he did it to. I told my mom and stepdad about it and they instantly went looking for him. They found him my mom's husband beat the guy up and then stole his truck.

When my mom died, he claimed that she took the truck and he covered for her in which that was not true. They both made the decision to go do that on that day so it is on both of them. He blamed my mom for that and was so angry at her after she died.

He made it very clear she was the reason he was in jail instead of mourning the loss of his wife. I don't know much of what happened for the two months I was gone but my siblings had told me things got so much worse. The treatment I got soon turned to them. The fighting got worse between my mom and her husband. In that time, I was gone there were 3 domestic disturbances between my mom and her husband.

On April 25th shortly after my birthday my mom came and got me in Cotopaxi. My siblings had gone back to Nebraska with my grandma a couple weeks after I left. As I said my mom's husband went to prison again so she was alone for about a month before I came back. When she came and picked me up, she was super tan and had honey blonde hair. I didn't ask her what she was doing while we were gone because I knew I would not get an answer. We got a hotel room in canon for the night and made our way to pueblo the next day. We got a hotel room in pueblo west and got it set up for my siblings to come a week later.

When my siblings returned everyone was excited to be back together again but by the end of the day everyone was arguing. It was hot and we were very unprepared to have my siblings but my mom did not want them gone any longer. We had a good two weeks together before my mom died. Things were much simpler and happier without my mom's husband there I must say. We got breakfast every morning in the hotel she would stay with us all night for the first week and then wake up with us and get breakfast with us. She would eat and get ready and leave for the day. We were content finally even if we were living in a hotel. As long as we had our mom and actually had her, we were happy. she was still getting high but not nearly as much as she used to.

It wasn't until the next week things started to get bad. She had told us that she had met a man who knew her father. He claimed he was best friends with him back in college. I didn't believe it to be true but she seemed very excited. She wanted us to meet him and one early morning at around 3 am she came into our room. We were all sleeping. I had just fallen asleep and she turned on the lamp and asked us to wake up.

We woke up and there was an older man I thought he was in his 60s he had all white hair and a white beard and he looked very old. He had on a leather jacket and he introduced himself to us. He seemed very stand offish and jittery he wouldn't look us in the eye. His demeanor didn't say much. As soon as we introduced ourselves, he was quick to leave. He had gotten a room next to us in our mom's name which I thought was very weird. She told us he had just gotten out of prison she had said he was somewhat famous.

He had been on the show called lockdown. Me and my mom used

to watch that show together. When she showed me the video, I was very concerned he looked like a maniac. Now I watch that video and I am even more sickened knowing that violent person took my mom's life also in a violent way and she was not the only one who's life he took. My mom had come back the next day and had told us that she had come across a huge opportunity. She claimed she had met a man who ran a gambling ring. She said they had tables for sale for 8,000 and she could make 10,000 on a good night. Many people were playing at these tables some who were doctors and lawyers from pueblo. She said that she was going to buy a table and all of our worries would soon be fixed. As long as this table did well. She said that she was going to go run a game

that night to test it out. It was the 17th of May. She got herself ready after talking to us about it. She took a shower put on her nicest outfit and did her makeup. She got ready to go, but she got a call. Her face instantly dropped after answering the call. She said she had to go and would be back soon, but she had no time to talk. She left about 3 PM. Later on, at 6 pm she returned. She was furious and frantically looking for her other phone. She had two phones one hers the other her husbands. I asked her what was going on because she was too worried for me not to ask.

She had said "you know that guy I had you guys meet the other day?" I said "yes?" she said "well he's a fucking piece of shit and stole the money I was going to use to buy the table with. She had $5,000 to put down on it. She then said there was another situation. She said that she had been tricked by the man into believing she was picking up guns for the cartel. I was so confused because I did not know she was involved in that again. She had said that he told her to go pick these guns up from this farm and give them to him. He was going to take them to his boss. What really happened is he set her up to steal these guns so he could pin it on her.

He sold those guns and the cartel found out. So, he was supposed to get them back and return them to the cartel. My mom said that was what she was going to do and that and that she was going to "handle this fool". She said she would be back in the morning. That was the last time I ever saw my mom alive again. My mom said that the man was waiting outside for her and that she needed to go. He was the last person she was seen alive with. I knew when she didn't come back the next day something was wrong.

The one thing that stuck out to me when she left is how she allowed us to hold onto her longer this time when we hugged her. She did not promise she would be back. She almost always promised she was going to be back. When we were last with mom, she agreed shed promise to tell us everything from then on because it was just us now.

I stayed up all night waiting for my mom and I fell asleep about 5 am. I woke up at 8 to get my sibling's breakfast. Our mom still was not back and I didn't have any calls or text messages. *She would've at least called by now to check in,* I thought to myself. My mom left $400 with me I didn't realize she did that until I opened the drawer next to me.

My heart sank. Everything started to feel wrong. Why did she leave me so much money? Why has she not checked in yet?" 11 o clock rolled around and still my mom's not answering her phone. By that time, I had called about 20 times since we woke up. I wasn't going to get another room just in case she was in jail or dead. I needed that money to take care of my siblings.

The front office called and asked if we would be checking out or staying another day. I went silent I didn't know what to do then. I just kept hearing mam, mam, are you there come back to me I said yes, I am, can you give us another hour and a half please its very needed. The lady agreed I started blowing my mom's phone up begging her to call me back I got a call back and some man answered the phone I said "hello? Mom where are you?

Were about to get kicked out." the man then said "who is this?" I said "I'm ambers daughter who is this?" and the man said his name I said "why do you have my mom's phone?" he said "uhm your mom will be back in a bit she just left but she left her phone here" I said "to where" he said "I don't know" I said "okay well have her call me back when she gets back, he said OK. 1:25 hits the front office hasn't called yet were packing our stuff up because

I knew my mom was not coming to get us. I called a taxi. The taxi costed $7.00 to come to us I knew this $400 was not going to last very long. I did not know what to do about everything going on. At 1:30 the front office calls and says we need to leave I said "my mom is not here yet please just give us another 30 minutes. The lady said I'm sorry but we've already given you two hours past check out time you guys have 7 minutes to get out of there because the police are coming. I said "why?" the lady said "because children cannot be left unattended by a parent or legal guardian and as you stated your mother is not there and hasn't been.

I hung up and told my siblings we need to leave immediately. We got our stuff and brought it outside luckily as soon as we got outside the taxi was pulling up.

As we got our last bag in the car the police pulled into the parking lot. I yelled at my siblings to get In and I told the driver to go, go, go! He did and we left the parking lot of the quality inn hotel where we were staying. The taxi driver then asked me what was going on. I told him and he said "oh my god! I'm so sorry you're going through this right now" he dropped us off at my brother's friend's house we didn't have anywhere else to go I called everyone I knew and so did he and finally his friend let us come over.

We were there for a couple hours and things were so hectic. I didn't know what to do my sister was throwing a huge fit because she was scared and didn't know what was going on. My brother tried to stay calm so did I but inside we both were freaking out. My brother's friend's dad and her brothers came home and they kicked us out which I don't blame them they did not expect 3 kids to be in their home when they got there. I got a hold of my cousin in law who we lived with when we first met my mom's husband. She let us come over but she wanted $300 in rent for the month I tried to explain that I only had $400 and we wouldn't even be there a whole month sure enough we were only there for a week.

I called the police from the very first day my mom went missing to put in missing person's report for her I told them her maiden name and her married name. Yet, they did not put out a report. The cops in fact told me when I called and asked them if they had put a missing person report out, they said yes. They told me they had officers out looking for her. I finally got a hold of my mom's husband and told him she was missing. It was on May 20th that he answered and he then put out a report himself. Me and my siblings went to my mom's mother-in-law to stay with her until we figured out what was going on with my mom.

On may 21st I got a call from the pueblo police department. A man said "hello? Is this Alexia Deck?" I said yes this is. He said we have information regarding your mother I am a detective from New Mexico I am here with my partner." I was skeptical at first. I thought it was a set up. Why did I think that? I don't know, but I had that thought in my head when I was on the phone with the man, even though the police themselves called me. I went to the courthouse with my grandmother in law. Two detectives were waiting at the door. They took me up to the third floor to an interrogation room.

We sat down and they began by saying they had located a woman's body in Pecos New Mexico. My stomach dropped. I thought my mom had done something wrong. She never killed anyone, though. I did not know what to expect from her anymore. Especially with how she was acting in the last seven months. I asked them who it was.

They said we have some questions to ask you first. They started asking me questions about my mom. They wanted to know where she was last seen. They wanted to know what time she left the motel. They sked me what she was wearing when she left. They asked who she was last seen with. Then they started asking me if she was involved in the cartel. I hesitated at first.

Then I said yes because I wanted to know what happened I wanted to know if my mom was okay or not. Any information would help they claimed.

I told them what she told me the night she left. It took 45 minutes of them asking me questions for them to then tell me "Well alexia we are sorry to inform you but the woman's body we found in New Mexico was identified as your mother." I felt my soul lift out of my body. I was blank. All I could hear was ringing in my ears. My senses came back. I asked them with pain in my voice "are you sure it's her?" They said yes, we identified her by her fingerprint records in the FBI database. She came up as Amber Deck. I still could not believe it. Then rage swept over me as a realized how long it took for them to tell me my mom was gone.

I asked them to tell me from the beginning, now felt so guilty for being mad at her. I thought she left us again but this time for good and that's why she never said anything and left us the $400. Either that or she had died, but I never thought she could die. She was my mom she was invincible she's survived the unthinkable. I asked them another question and their answer will forever burn in my mind as their answer was a lie. I asked if my mom suffered and they both said "No, the first bullet hit her heart she died instantly." Yet that was not true! I would come to find out much later.

Due to the fact they took so long to tell me and I had also just learned my mother was dead, I freaked out. I was overwhelmed and I started crying hysterically. I left the room. As I left the interrogation room, there were approximately 15 cops out in the hallway.

There was a Sargant and the chief. One of the police told me to calm down. I snapped I said "calm down? Calm down? I just learned my mother was murdered and it took 45 minutes for anyone to tell me. I've been alone in this. You guys have not helped matters. Instead, you have made them worse. Yet you're telling me to calm down?" They were all staring at me. Two cops started to laugh at me. I turned to them and I said "do you have wives? Is your mother still alive? Do you have children" they both said yes to all my questions I then said "so how would you feel if you were to find out that your wife or daughter or mother had been murdered yet no one told you anything.

How would you feel if all the police did was laugh at you? How the fuck would you feel?" they both just put their heads down. I had to get out of there. It was hard to breathe. I felt as though someone was suffocating me. I ran down the stairs and out the door leading outside and I ran across the street and just screamed "NOOOO WHYYY"

My mom's mother-in-law was a little way behind me she walked to me and hugged me. I just wanted to rip my skin off. I didn't want her or anyone touching me. I wanted to run away, but to where?

I composed myself and the New Mexico investigators walked up. They said "we are so sorry for your loss" I was so angry at everything I said to them "no you're not! You don't care" I was speaking out of anger and grief, but those two men, I have to say were the only ones who cared. The whole time my mom was missing, and up until I left Colorado and came back home to my family in Nebraska, is a blur.

I don't remember much of what happened. After that I was in shock. I just remember we left and my grandmother in law took me back to my cousin in laws house where my siblings were. I did not know how to tell them nor did I want to tell them.

They were so hopeful that our mom was going to come back to us. I first went and told my cousin in law so she was aware my siblings might break down. All she had said to me was "I'm sorry, but when you tell your siblings make sure your sister doesn't scream or break anything or you guys will have to leave!" I thought about leaving right then and there but we had nowhere to go and I had just given her $300. She wasn't going to give it back as it had already gone to her bills.

I worked up the courage after dinner to tell my siblings the news. I wanted them to eat first for comfort. I sat them down and my cousin and her boyfriend went upstairs to give us space. I told them the news of or moms passing and they did not react how I expected them to. My brother didn't say a word he just stared at me with no expression on his face except a tear that welled up and fell down his cheek.

Same with my sister she did not say anything she just stared at me but she did not shed a single tear. I was confused as to why they did not react how I expected but then it dawned on me that they did not feel comfortable enough in their house to react. They did not know these people and they were also in shock.

So, I decided we should take a walk and maybe that might help. We were a few streets away from our old house.

I decided to go to the library I knew it was down the street. It was about 8 o clock at the time. We walked in silence to the library and when we got there, we sat down on the curb in the parking lot. I asked them how they felt and they said they felt okay but were confused. I explained to them a little more in detail about what I knew. I didn't know much I just knew that the man she left with had to have done it. They agreed it had to have been him. We sat in silence for a little longer they didn't really know what to say or how to react. I understood how they felt.

Part of them believed she was still alive as did I. We thought she just faked her death and she would come back eventually. We kept that hope for a while. Me and my siblings went back to our cousin in laws house and I decided that night I would call our grandmother in law to come take my siblings. We weren't on the best of terms.

I had not really spoken to her or seen her since I got kicked out of her house. She had driven me to the police station about my mom but that was it really. I decided not to go and that I would try and make it work at my cousins. It did but I needed to be with my siblings and they needed me so 4 days later I had my grandmother in law pick me up. She allowed me to come back. While living there they tried to blame our mom for everything that went wrong.

They constantly brought up the fact she made a lot of mistakes. Was that supposed to make us feel better? All they wanted to do was point out what "she had done" in the past. They brought up the quinceañera situation. They went on, and on. To everyone else they would talk about how they loved my mom and missed her.

They tried to make other people see how much love they felt for us kids. They even tried to buy our love. All while belittling our late mother.

On May 25th I got a hold of my grandma aka my mom's mom and so did my brother to ask for her address. I did not have the heart to tell her that her daughter had passed away. I knew she would feel worse pain than I did as the eldest daughter. I regret not telling her. It did not help having my decision swayed by my grandmother in law.

I asked her if I should tell my grandma about my mom or have the cops go and tell her to make it easier. I don't know why I thought it would make it easier having the cops tell my grandma. She told me I should have a cop go over there as well as a priest. I was not in the right mindset so I agreed and called them. They agreed to go and inform my grandma. I waited for her to call me.

She did not that day which I did not expect her to. After doing that I realized what I had done and I felt horrible because I should've been the one to tell her not some strangers. My grandma wanted to come and get all of us and she had called my siblings school and told them she was going to come and get us.

The school then called my grandmother in law and she told me so I got ahold of my grandma and told her not to come. I was angry at the world at everything so I took it out on my grandma but that did not stop her from coming. I am so grateful that she never gave up.

My grandmother in law was then worried my grandma would come and get the kids so she decided she wanted to take my sister to my grandmother in laws mother-in-law to hide her. It was two and a half hours away from where we were living. I told her I didn't think my grandma would come and that we should wait. Secretly I was hoping my grandma would come.

There was a little part of me who wanted to just be back home with my grandma and have my siblings there because I knew we'd be safe but for a while I let pride get in the way of that. Since my mom was gone, I felt it was my duty to do everything myself. Another part of me felt that since I was an adult my grandma wouldn't want me to come and shed take my siblings from me. The thought of that scared me but it wasn't the case. In my mind me and my siblings were now my responsibility and mine alone.

About a week later my grandma came and got my siblings, she did not tell anyone she was coming and one morning we woke up to our grandmother in law telling us to get up the cops were downstairs. Me and my sister got up right away and started freaking out. We went downstairs and there was a cop and a detective standing in the living room.

They explained that my grandma was there to get us and told us my grandma and grandpa were waiting at the police station and that we had to come it was court ordered. My grandmother in law went to talk to the detective and when they came back the detective said "can you guys go pack up your stuff" so we all went to pack and when we came back down the detective said to me "wait, your grandma has said she does not want you to come. She is just here for your siblings you're 18 now and an adult so you can fend for yourself. I'm sorry but you have to stay." I and my siblings were so confused. That didn't sound like that grandma we knew. My siblings got ready to leave and my grandmother in law walked to the door opened it and told them "Do not tell anyone anything we will come and get you guys back" my siblings were crying because they didn't want to leave but it was truly for the best.

When my siblings got to the police department my grandma was shocked that I was not with them because before the cop and detective left to get my siblings my grandma specifically had told them to ask me if I wanted to come as well. My grandma did want me to come and they lied to me. The cops never once asked me if I wanted to come with them.

My grandmother in law waited for my stepdad to call and she told him the news. They decided to try and fight for custody of my siblings. My mom did give power of attorney to my grandmother in law and stepdad so they had a chance to fight for custody. My stepdad was still in prison at the time and would not be getting out until December. He gave all rights to his mother including the rights to my mom's body.

My grandma and I both called the funeral home where my mom was located and asked for her body and for her not to be cremated, we specifically said that many times. I also asked for the pictures to my mom's autopsy to see what really happened to her. I had a feeling more had happened and they continually told me no and then told me that her body was far too gone for pictures to be taken. I had been asking for a month. Moms body was at the funeral home for 2 months before we got her back in ashes. They said her body was too far gone by the time they finally said we can have her back and that she needed to be cremated. I was even more angry because of that and when it was time to go get my mom my grandmother in law told me I could not come with.

I got lost in my mom's death from the day. I found out about 6 months ago I was detached from myself. It was as if I was on autopilot. I buried myself in work and school I was supposed to have graduated a week after my mom died, but I could not go finish school. I went back the next year and graduated although it wasn't for myself it was for my mom. She wanted more than anything to see me graduate so I did. As soon as I graduated, I went back to Nebraska. All I wanted was to graduate and go back home to my family. I was away from them for a year and a half after my mom died, I almost broke without them.

The whole time during my mom's case I was not allowed to go

to any of the court preceding's. I was a witness according to the witness advocate who in fact did nothing for us but make matters worse. I called every week to check up on the case. I was told I was not allowed to know anything after the court dates when I called to ask for an update.

I was told again and again I was not allowed to know anything. I never got to testify to anything. Everything I told the investigators was put into the court records. Instead, they put everything the killer and the accomplice said gave them both a chance to speak for themselves but my mom did not have that chance we were her advocates we were her voice and we were denied that from everyone in the law enforcement and court.

The media also lied and made my mom look like she deserved to die. She was made to look like she was a criminal and the guy who killed her was doing society a favor. My mom was a good person she helped a lot of people even when they didn't deserve it. She never asked for anything in return. She made bad decisions. She did hurt people in the process, but as humans we do that. We make mistakes and we hurt people especially when we're hurting ourselves. It makes me so mad that so many people took the opportunity to tarnish my mom's name after her death.

Like they didn't make the same mistakes or worse. At least my mom tried to make up for her mistakes and do better. Before she died, she wanted to stop everything. She was done. She had finally come to her senses, and that last job was supposed to be our ticket out of that life. She was also going to divorce her husband and she had told him in an argument when she was angry. I overheard him say "if you try and divorce me, I will kill you." My mom knew I heard him say that and went out to the car to talk to him and 15 minutes later I went to check on her and she was crying.

I asked her what was wrong and she told me "Things will always be this way well never get out of this I'm so tired of everything I just want to go back home to Nebraska and start all over but I can't I can never go back" I felt so bad for my mom. We scraped by every day and many people blame my mom for our misfortune and suffering but in all reality, it was the people she loved and were in trusted positions that turned their back on her, stole from her, used her, abused her and she did best with what she had. Yes, she could've asked for help but when you really think of it not many of us are inept to sharing our feelings and asking for help and my mom was not one to do either. She would truly rather struggle than put her burdens so she called it onto others because it was her mess. That is what she told me.

If the world had not been so cruel maybe my mom would still be alive maybe if the system had kept my mom's killer in prison like he should've been then maybe my mom might still be alive. One of the first things people said when my mom died and the news published an article was "what was the motive?" as if that is a valid reason to take another's life. My mom had done no harm to anyone she did not deserve to die it was not her fault it was not the guns fault it was simply the person who pulled the trigger and decided to take a person's life that was at fault.

Yet everyone blamed the victim because of her criminal background. But what about her background of the help she gave to people? The cold cases she cracked that the police themselves could not figure out. although my mom could not escape the life she chose once upon a time she made do with it and used that to bring down actual bad people who were doing harm. My mom did not have one violent charge on her record so why was she sought out to be such a bad person in her death?

At the same time many people spoke of amazing things about my mom many did respect and love her many knew of my mom but very little knew who my mom truly was. And for that I am here to speak on her behalf to show the world who my mom truly was.

SECOND TO THE OLDEST DAUGHTER'S STORY

Amber's second daughter's story begins at her birth, but her life was much more complicated than this simple birth announcement from the North Platte Telegraph. "Amber and Lance Deck of North Platte are the parents of a daughter, Athena, born late July, 2004, weighing six pounds, nine ounces. Her grandparents are Carol and Trevor from England, and Ladonna and Dino and Donald, all from North Platte." Athena's adoption nearly destroyed the relationship between myself and Amber because of my past adoption. I stopped talking to Amber for almost an entire year.

That was a horrible time. She was ashamed and I was angry that she did to her daughter what my mother did to me. Had Amber told me the truth about what was going on in her life, I could have and would have saved Athena from being adopted. Amber believed she was doing the right thing by giving Athena up for adoption. She believed she was saving her daughter from a hard life. Ultimately, Amber should have listened to me when I told her to leave her husband. Had she listened, she would never have lost Athena. I could have helped her, but I did not know the entire truth.

Amber did spare Athena a lot of grief. Sometimes, parents are forced to accept things they do not want to accept. As Amber's mother, I accepted many things I never dreamed of accepting. Athena leaving our family was the hardest thing our family had ever gone through. None of us knew the toll Athena's adoption was going to have on Amber. Amber did leave her husband because she could not live with her choice of staying with him.

She blamed him for losing Athena. Amber had every right to blame Lance.

He began the destructive behavior that sent Amber in the direction of self-medication via drugs. He was the one who introduced Amber to Methamphetamine, otherwise known as meth. Meth is a powerful, highly addictive stimulant that affects the central nervous system. Lance used this to control Amber. By the time Amber told me she was addicted to meth, she was in over her head.

She tried so many times to break free of her addiction, but every choice she made in men led her deeper down the wrong path. It also led her further and further from the hurt she wanted to fix. Amber always wanted to tell her daughter why she gave her up. She wanted to tell her that handing her over to complete strangers was the hardest thing she ever did. Right up to the week before she was murdered, Amber looked for Athena. Giving up Athena was Amber's biggest regret!

HOW ATHENA FEELS OVER THE LOSS OF HER BIRTH MOTHER!

"When I was a baby Amber put me up for adoption. She was protecting me. I was taken into a new home when I was 13 months old. I had a good childhood. Every time I asked about my birth parents, I would get just her name. Amber, I knew she was young when she had me but that is all I knew. It was my dream to meet her.

My whole life I have thought about finding her. Yes, that thought was a little scary. What if she did not want me or what if I have siblings? I was scared but I knew I wanted to find her. My mom always said that she would help me find her when I was old enough. It was around the end of march, 2022 when I found out she passed away.

It broke me into a million pieces. I cried on the stairs unable to move, unable to breathe. All I could do was cry. It felt like my whole life was just taken away from me, my dreams crushed. I was filled with anger, confusion, numbness, and depression, it was all so much. I did not know how to take it. Who could do this to someone? Especially a sweet loving mother like Amber. I then looked up the story my parents told me and found her last name and then I went to Facebook. I found her and contacted people who were friends with her and that is how I found Carol, my grandma. Then I found out I have four siblings which was just music to my ears. I am so grateful I found them even though it was through a complicated process. I am amazed that I found them.

I know I did not personally know Amber, but she was still my mom and I still loved her and missed her every day. I wanted nothing more than to meet her and that opportunity was ripped away from me. It honestly feels like I will never be whole. I will never really know who I am. I had so many questions and things to tell her. I know she never gave up on me and I never gave up on her. I tried so hard my whole life to find her but did not have enough information.

I love you mama and I am so sorry this happened to you. I wish I could have at least given you one hug or heard your voice even one time. I will never forget you!"

As an adoptee, I know how Athena feels. She cannot ever feel Amber's big ole hugs. She is too young to remember those. It was Amber who took care of Athena, not Lance. It was Amber's voice Athena responded to. I honestly do not know why Lance was the way he was.

He was not a good person to anyone except his and Amber's first daughter.

Amber loved children. When our family lost Athena, we lost Amber as well. She was never the same. She never found her way out of the grief she felt having to give up her baby girl.

Amber was my baby girl. I could not stay angry at her forever. I can honestly say that Amber was a good soul mixed up in a mind full of regrets. Even on her worse days she would help someone in need. However, Amber did get herself mixed up with the wrong kind of people. That came many years after the loss of Athena.

AMBER'S ONLY SON'S STORY

Amber's only sons story begins at his conception. Amber married her second husband. He is Native American. Her second husband went to school with her big sister who was a year older than Amber. He was born from the couple's love for each other. Amber's husband asked her if she wanted to have his baby. Amber said yes. Her son was born late August.

Her son does not remember who he lived with during his early years. I am not sure he remembers his early years at all. He might or might not have random memories that pop into his head, but he chooses not to talk about it. By her sons' birth, his father was already getting into more trouble than his worth. Amber struggled with her troubles. She left her eldest daughter with her father more than she cared for her, and she left her son with me.

He was a few months old when my husband and I decided to buy him a crib and put him in our room. Amber had her eldest daughter push his bassinet out to the living room one early morning. Amber did not want to get up for him because she had been out all night. I do not know how long he had been out in the living room by himself, but by the time I heard him, he was crying uncontrollably. It took me at least 20 mins of comforting and a complete bedding change to calm him down. I was furious with Amber, and at the same time I felt so bad for her son. He was just a baby. So, I made sure he never had to experience that treatment again.

Amber did not seem to mind. She was gone more than she was home. Even after Amber moved herself and her eldest daughter into a place of their own, her son stayed with me. It was like I was his mother and Amber was his aunt, or his big sister. She would pick him up for outings then bring him home to me. Not take him home with her.

I became grandma, mommy. Amber's son was a busy little boy, and such a happy guy. Amber missed out on his first steps, and everything else. He called me ma, ma, ma. His favorite thing to do was growling into my neck. Amber set up doctor appointments for her son, and school when he reached school age, but he did not live with her. The address on his school records was mine and his grandpa's. Amber simply could not be his mother.

I believe it was because of how her sons father treated her and how he let her down. Ambers second marriage ended as abruptly as it began with baby Zay at a loss over both his parents. He never gave up on his parents. He got excited when they came to get him. I don't know if his excitement was because he was going on an outing, or that he knew his parents were his parents. I am sure it was confusing for such a little guy, but I did my best to keep him occupied, and comforted him.

Amber's son and his grandpa had as special a bond as he and I did. When his emotions were hurt, he wanted me. When he got ill, or physically hurt he wanted grandpa. He was specific as to who he wanted for what reasons. Play time was for his mommy and he did eventually call Amber mommy. Amber called him brother boy. To me, he was my little busy Izzy.

It has to be confusing at any age, to know that both your parents abandoned you. Both of his parents had many chances to prove that they cared for him. Mom and dad proved that the only love they had for him was the placement they both chose for him. My grandson has been primarily in my care since a week after his birth.

Aside from random 1 AM visits, his father never came around. The poor little guy only saw his mother on rare occasions. Amber's son did finish kindergarten at his mother's home, but he also spent every weekend at our home. He didn't get much time then to spend with his mother. He spent a few short months with his mother and siblings during summer, then moved in with grandpa and I full time. he spent 4 school years with us before mom insisted all the children be with her in Pueblo Colorado.

How does Amber's son feel about his mother's death?

He feels like his mother abandoned him. He doesn't want to talk about it. He knows that his grandpa and grandma love him and support him, and he knows we always have, and will. I am pretty sure that he feels that both his parents could have and should have shown him more love.

He wishes that he could have had what others do. He wishes he could have had more time with his mother. He feels that his mother put herself in harm's way more times than not. He does not feel that his mother deserved to die, especially the way she died. He feels like his mother did a lot of bad things. Amber was his mother, and he does love her, but he will never know how much she loved him. This is life at its most unfairness.

SECOND YOUNGEST DAUGHTER'S STORY

She was born a Cervantes in late September. Less than 4 months after her birth her father took Amber to court for custody. She then became a Flores. Amber was in jail several times, for various reasons which I do not know. I do believe that Amber used Meth while pregnant with her daughter, but as she was in jail a lot, access was cut off and she received regular medical visits while in jail. She was Amber's first C section delivery. Amber had been out of jail for several months before she was born.

Amber was seeing a new man when her daughter was born. Amber gave her the new boyfriends surname in the hopes that her birth father would be deterred from claiming her. The name did not deter him. When Amber was supposed to go to custody court over her, Amber did not go. That is how and why her father won custody.

I was going to go to court with Amber, but she told me to stay out of it. She has been in the care of her step mother since she was 4 months old. Her step mother refused my repeated requests to have her come for visits even after Amber's death. She gets into trouble when her step mother finds out she has communications with me.

I know what kind of life she had, but I can not comment on the life she had aside from this……

I know that if she had the choice, she would have chosen both sides of her family. I do think that she wanted to be with her mother. She loved her mother very much.

WHAT SHE SAYS ABOUT HER MOTHER.

"The one thing I miss the most about my mom is her hugs. When she hugged me, I got a warm safe feeling knowing that would always be safe in her arms and that always gave me comfort.

The last time I saw my mom was a week before she passed so I don't really remember her voice that much but I remember when we were at a store and she told my siblings we couldn't get any candy since we hadn't had supper yet but I asked her for candy and she said yes anything for my princess. And after that I still know I'm the favorite.

One thing that would make her laugh is when I'd get really sassy and tell my brother the leave me the heck alone and she would say oh yeah, you're definitely my baby girl!

A way I will always think of when I remember my mom is the way she loved everyone ♥

She had to overcome motherhood and marriage."

YOUNGEST DAUGHTERS STORY

Amber's youngest was born late June. We do not know for certain who her father is. Amber took that secret to her grave. We have done DNA testing and are waiting on results.

Before her birth, Amber was using Meth whenever she could get her hands on it. This was not good for Amber's youngest daughter. Her mother's addiction became her addiction. Unfortunately, For Ambers youngest her mother manipulated authorities into believing that she was clean throughout her pregnancy. She wasn't clean.

Years later Amber's eldest daughter and her only son, told stories of how their mother used them to pass her urine tests. Amber's eldest daughter even asked me what she should do. I told my eldest granddaughter to let her mom know that grandma knew what she was doing, and that it was wrong of her to use them. Being put on the spot stopped Amber from using her children to pass her drug tests. It didn't stop her though. She found other people to use.

Amber's youngest spent the first 3 years of her life with her mother and older sister. Her older sister took care of her more than her mother did. Yes, even as a baby, big sister was more of a mother to her than her mother. Thankfully, the youngest was a fairly calm baby.

From 3 years to 8 years, I spent every day taking care of Amber's youngest. I did have about 7 months reprieve, that really didn't help. Her youngest has developmental issues due to Amber not being there for her. Amber's eldest daughter was merely a child herself. By this time Amber was well into drugs. So far into drugs that her youngest became her princess that could do no wrong. When anyone tried to tell her youngest not to do something,

Amber told her she didn't have to listen. Her youngest was 3 years old and becoming so confused.

I recall a time when Amber was napping on our couch in the Livingroom. She had been there a while. It was the middle of the afternoon. Amber's youngest got home from preschool. She saw her mom napping and tried to climb up to snuggle her. Amber shoved her off the couch, got up and left. She was gone for days. Amber's little princess's face was a mixture of sadness and pain. She thought she did something to make her mom leave.

Her now 10-year-old mind is maturing more every day. It seems like a year ago she was 3. That is how she acted. She is doing better this year at school. She did struggle with d's and f's where she is now a straight A student with behavior issues that are slowly going away.

HOW DOES AMBER'S YOUNGEST DAUGHTER FEEL ABOUT THE MURDER OF HER MOTHER?

She was devastated and took it out on me. She argued with me on a daily basis. She has learned how to grow. How to accept responsibility for her actions, and how to be nice to others. She has more tendencies of her mother than her siblings. She goes to counseling that began as a weekly session and is now every 3 weeks. She has finally come to terms that her mother is actually gone. She did not want to believe anyone. She watched and patiently waited for her mother to come home. That day will never come. Amber was cremated and we all have her ashes at home.

DADDY'S STORY

In 2001 I married an English man. My husband is the only father Amber ever knew. Her biological father died when Amber was around 4 years old. Amber was 13 when my husband and I started seeing each other. None of my children were sure if they wanted to call my husband dad, let alone accept him. One of my husbands' fondest memories of Amber was she called him daddy. He thought of her as his own. Amber was the first of my children to accept him as her daddy. He also loved her smile. One of Ambers greatest features. Her smile lit up the room.

Despite her insecurities, Amber made friends easily. All she had to do was smile. When she figured that out the world was indeed hers for the taking. She used her smile to get what she wanted. Sometimes that was good, but other times it was not so great. Where Amber was concerned, there are many mixed emotions. She was an act first then deal with the consequences later type of person. Her addiction to drugs amplified this issue. Amber did not like having to deal with her actions.

I spent a lot of time with Amber because she was my youngest child. She picked up many great habits from me, like her love of old music. This was another of those things Amber's daddy loved about her. Her taste in music. She would get in his car, and not complain about his music. She loved to sing, and knew the lyrics! Amber and her daddy also shared a love for books. He would chat with her about what he was reading, she would say, "That sounds like an amazing read! Can I read it when your done?"

I personally do not have a mathematical mind, but my husband and Amber do. I am sure that my husband misses the little math matches he and Amber got into. He misses her hugs too! I always knew when Amber was upset with me. She would come into the room and hug daddy first. I would not get the hug! I only received a half smile when she was upset with me. Daddy was Ambers go to person especially if she was pissy with me. She was pissy with me a lot, because I was the enforcer, not daddy. Her daddy rarely got angry with her. There were times, but those times were few and far between.

Amber was our first child to give us grandchildren. Though she was too young to have children and not at all mature enough to have children, she had them first. She gave us our first granddaughter when she was 14. She got pregnant while she was on vacation with her sister. She married the man that got her pregnant. Amber forced us to accept many things. Our grandchildren are the best of those forces. My husband loves being a grandpa. Our grandchildren keep him young, and very busy.

The only negative thing Amber's daddy had to say was that despite all the help we gave her, Amber refused to help herself. As Ambers addiction took hold of her, we essentially enabled her. We protected our grandchildren from the life she was placing them in. That allowed her to do whatever she wanted to do. She knew her children were safe with us. It was frustrating for us because Amber would drop off children and say she would be back in a bit. When I would call her, she would tell me she was just past Brady. That little Amber saying has become a joke for our family. Where is she this time, my husband would ask. I would reply with she's just past Brady! Two weeks later she came through the door. Brady was about 30 to 40 minutes away.

My husband came into a ready-made family. He did not know if he would be accepted. He had no clue what he was in for. He came from a single child English family. I did try to warn him, because I could see that my Amber was going to be a challenge. He joined us anyway, and has never looked back. He stuck by my side through everything Amber put us through. Every time Amber got herself into trouble her car would get impounded. Every time her car got impounded daddy went to get it out. He knew full well that he would go back in a month or a few days to get it out again, but he told her off and repeated the cycle. I know he hoped for the best for his little girl. The ending she received was not the ending any of us expected. Especially her daddy.

MOMMA'S STORY

Being Amber's mother was a challenge and blessing all rolled up in a nice sometimes stressful Amber package. A piece of amber is a rough fossilized resin that can be polished up into a beautiful gem. That was my Amber. She was my rough unpolished gem. I was going to name her Angel, but the mother sharing my hospital room named her daughter Angel. I am happy with Amber it suited my girl perfectly. Amber's middle name came from me.

As a baby Amber was as perfect as any little girl could be. She only cried when she was fighting her sleep, hungry, or needed changed. She rarely got sick. The only time Amber was seriously ill she was a month old and her sister was a year and a month. Big sister had bronchial pneumonia and Amber had pneumonia. They both spent about a week in the hospital. Neither girl ever got that sick again. I am pretty sure they caught their illness from their big brothers and their ages amplified the regular cold.

Ambers big brother and I taught her how to walk. As a toddler she never wanted for anything. She only had to whine, point and any one of her older siblings would get whatever she wanted. Amber's big brothers wanted to take her everywhere with them. I would not allow it until Amber was over 5 years old. Part of that reason was because I had no idea where her father was until Social Security informed me of his death. Amber was 4 at that time. Her father had tried once to steal her. I was not having a repeat of that.

In grade school Amber and her sister were my straight A children. Both girls joined band, choir, and Amber tried sports. She like basketball, and wrestling. She did not like them long enough to stick with them. At the age Amber's son is now, 13, she began looking at older men. I did not know that until I uprooted my daughters to move to England. My boys were old enough by then to be on their own. I also had my best friend and my adopted father looking over the boys to make sure they were doing alright.

Taking care of 5 growing children as a single parent is no easy feat. Growing up is not easy for anyone. Even the richest of the rich kids struggle with adolescence. Amber struggled just as much or more than any other child her age. The difference is that Amber never really answered for what she did because she always had me protecting her. Ultimately, I began enabling Amber way before she involved herself in drugs. I never allowed her to have to answer for her mistakes. I was too busy working to notice that Amber had some serious issues that I should have not ignored.

That is the purpose of this book. I want to point out the issues parents should look for. All those tale tale signs that something is not right. If you take the time to read this book Amber's mistakes can help you see the right way to go. That is after all what Amber wanted. She wanted to fix everything. She could not though. Amber got in way to deep. Amber was never a bad person!

No matter how deep my daughter got herself in, I never gave up on her. I loved her to the moon and beyond. She will always be in my heart, and I will continue to help her children get past everything she put herself through. No one ever said that being a parent would be easy. Personally, I would do it all again. Heck, I am doing it all again. This time I will do it right.

If you are interested in reading about Amber and her sisters' shenanigans, her sister wrote a book about them. Forbidden Love can be found on Amazon.

CHAPTER ONE
Moms missing, Grandma!

April 29th, 2021, I began a trip to Colorado to welcome my newest grandson and help with my eldest daughter's young ones. My eldest daughter had an emergency C section for my fifth grandson. I did not want to take Amber's youngest to her, but I had no choice. I could not go to Colorado and not allow Amber to at least see her children. At the seeing her children point, she would have insisted they stay with her.

We were supposed to meet Amber in Pueblo, but I knew that would change. My daughter never stuck with anything, which caused me to run everywhere while trying to find where she was.

We were outside of Pueblo when Ambers only son called his mother. She told us to go on to Canon City, she would see us there, most likely shortly after we got there. She claimed that she was just getting ready to pick up her eldest daughter, then she would head to Canon City. She promised. Amber did not actually make it to Canon City until around supper time. Amber met me in the parking lot at IHOP in Canyon City. We were supposed to have a nice family meal. That did not happen either. I received the last big hug I would ever receive from my daughter.

I reluctantly handed over Ambers two youngest children to her so I could stay and help her big sister. My grandchildren were always happy to see and be with their mom. They always acted differently when with her. It was like they no longer had to respect me.

The two youngest were supposed to return to Nebraska and school. I should have picked them up on Sunday, but when Sunday came, I could not get ahold of Amber. My eldest daughter was comfortable taking care of the new baby. She was able to move around well, and she did have other family members to help her. I bought McDonalds breakfast for the bunch I was leaving and headed to the donut shop to pick up breakfast for Amber's kiddos.

As I headed down the highway, I hoped that Amber would contact me, before I reached Pueblo. Her call came through on the outskirts of Pueblo. She did not want me to come get the kids, but she would take the donuts for them. I met her in the parking lot of the motel. It was basically a drive by donut drop. She wanted to go back in before the kiddos woke up. That was the final time I saw my daughter alive, and the last Love you Momma I ever heard.

Right then, in that moment, Amber had the opportunity to send her children back with me. If she knew she was in trouble she could have loaded everyone into my car and I would have taken everyone home. I called my husband to let him know I was on my way home alone. Yes, we were both concerned, but we knew from experience that there was nothing we could do until Amber needed us again.

May 17th Amber sent me a message. She wanted 500 dollars for her eldest daughter's graduation party. Her daddy told me to tell her 100 dollars and gifts were enough for graduation. If only I had known why she needed money and how much she really needed.

Her eldest daughter told me that on May 17th she had not made plans for a weekend graduation party. Which led me to believe that Amber wanted 500 dollars to leave Pueblo. Which in turn told me that she knew she was going to die.

May 21st, 2021 Amber's eldest daughter messaged me to see if her mother had contacted me. "Mom's missing, grandma, and I think something bad has happened to her." I told her I heard nothing from her mother. I also tried to console my granddaughter by telling her that mom has been gone before and she always comes home. Boy, was I wrong. Right after I replied to my granddaughters' message, my dryer began beeping morse code style. I went to the living room to have my morning coffee. The next few days I felt drained. Every time I entered my laundry room my dryer began beeping like crazy. I unplugged the dryer. I seriously thought I was going nuts. I sure wish I knew morse code.

May 25th Amber's son and her eldest daughter messaged me. One by phone, the other by messenger. It drove me crazy because both children had my number. Neither of them would respond after I replied. I did not know exactly what was going on yet, but I had my suspicions. Those suspicions became evident after the sheriff showed up with a local pastor.

A few moments after my husband got home, and I told him what I had just experienced, both our phones rang. His phone rang first. He did not know the number so he did not answer. I answered my phone because I wanted to know who was calling both of us. I recognized the caller's voice. The person calling was one of Amber's old acquaintances. I had questions for her. *How did you get our numbers, and how did you find out about Amber's death so quickly?* She did not stay on the phone long. She offered her condolences and told me if there was anything she could do, to ask.

She told me that the news of Amber's death was all over social media. She claimed that was how she knew. The news on social media was about an unknown woman with no image and no name because the death was suspicious and the police were investigating. Amber's acquaintance claimed that she got our numbers from one of Amber's daughters' step mom. The problem with that was the step mom did not have our number's, and the step mom found out from Amber's eldest daughter after the acquaintance called us. So, how did she find out about Amber's death before anyone else knew?

The next day I had to silence my Facebook messenger because my phone was notifying me of messages from people I did not even know and people who knew I was Amber's mother. Two of those people were Amber's ex boyfriends. One of them was the father of one of Amber's daughters. There was no way I wanted to speak to anyone at all and I did not know what happened to my daughter. In that time, I only knew my daughter was murdered. Nothing more.

The third day after I found out about Amber's murder the principle from the kid's school called me. The last time I checked up on the kids progress in Pueblo schools I told the principle to call me if he had any problems over my grandchildren. He did just that. He called to clear things up and figure out what we were going to do about Amber's children. My grandson told the principle that their mom had been in a horrible accident. My granddaughter told him their mom had died. The principle called the jail and spoke to the kids step dad. He told the principle that Amber had been in a terrible car accident and she was in the hospital. Why would he lie about something like that? What was the point?

I explained that my granddaughter was telling the truth. I received the news of my daughter's death 2 days earlier. We discussed me heading to Pueblo to pick up the kids. I got off the phone. Put a few things together, got in my car and headed towards the interstate. I was on the onramp when the principle called back. He hoped I wasn't on my way yet, but I was. He told me the police took my grandchildren to the step grandmother. We talked for while I drove to the first exit. I headed home to phone the Pueblo Police. The principle seemed agitated that Amber added her step mother to the kid's emergency contact. He told me that was not a good place for my grandchildren to be. What did he know that he wasn't telling me?

When I got back home, I phoned the police department to begin what proved to be a very expensive battle for the grandchildren that I had been taking care of almost their entire lives. The police captain spoke to me for maybe an hour. He told me my grandchildren did not belong where they were. They needed their grandma. I agreed 100% He told me all I had to do was get a Pueblo judge to sign an emergency custody form so I could come pick up my grandchildren. If I could do that the captain would do everything in his power to get the kids away from Amber's in laws.

That conversation led me to look for a lawyer that wasn't from Pueblo. The captain told me I could not just come pick up my grandchildren. I had to take Amber's mother-in-law, and husband to court to get custody of my grandchildren. I called lawyer after lawyer. Explained the situation over and over. The next day Marrison's family law returned my phone call. They would begin our custody case after we paid 3 thousand dollars retainer fee. We paid the fee the very next day! The battle began, and it proved not to be as simple as the captain said.

Ambers in laws could have handed the children over to me, but they did not like me. They also had big plans for my grandchildren. Ambers in laws were a part of the same gang their son was a part of, but I discovered that much later. They accused me of all sorts of crazy crap. Some of their claims were that I abused my youngest granddaughter. They had absolutely no evidence, and no one to verify I was abusive to anyone. My youngest granddaughter denied their claims, and asked to go home to me.

The current husband claimed to have my grandchildren for two years. I immediately had the school fax the kids record to my lawyer. While in my care, Amber's children were in school every day. Her son was a straight A student. Her daughter was close to straight A's. I had Dr. visit documentation and dentist visit documentation. Amber sent me an eviction notice in November of 2020 that was in her husband's name. I used it against her husband. That proved he did not take care of the children and in fact did not pay his bills to keep a roof over their heads. Amber's husband was also in jail when she was murdered. He went to jail in April. So, how can you take care of children from jail? His mother took the children after Amber died, and only because the school got the police involved.

Amber's mother-in-law in fact, refused to help Amber while she was alive. That is why Amber stayed in a motel with her children and the children were with their big sister in that same motel until they ran out of paid motel time. From there they went to other members of Ambers husband, who did not help. They took the last of the money Amber's eldest daughter had, and made the kids lives miserable. So, please tell me again how much Amber's in laws took care of my grandchildren!

When our lawyer received the children's school records from Parkview Elementary School, this was the response from them. *Carol – Wanted to let you know we got the information from Park View in Pueblo regarding the kids. It's honestly pretty pathetic – out of 150 school days the kids were absent 24 and tardy 50!!!!!* So, I ask again, how is this taking care of Amber's children?

On June 23rd, 2021 we proved enough to the judge, and he granted us emergency custody of our grandchildren. We were not finished with court yet, but we were able to get our grandchildren away from the horrible situation they were in. Our granddaughter's 9th birthday was the 18th of June. We wanted to have emergency custody by her birthday, but it did not work out for us. I went to Colorado Springs to meet our lawyer and prove we were serious about getting our grandchildren.

I stayed a week in a motel that was near the law firm. My husband came a few days later to support my efforts of getting our grandchildren. On June 25th we decided to head home for the weekend, and get fresh clothes. We did not have the kids yet, but it didn't look like we were going to have them before the weekend. We gassed up both cars, and my husband led the way down highway 24 towards Limon Colorado. A storm popped up out of nowhere. Seriously, in my 57 years, I had never seen anything like it. It was as if Amber was telling me there is no way you're going to leave here without my kid's momma! That's when the lawyer called, and I pulled over to answer his call.

He asked me if we had left yet, and I told him we had just gassed up and were heading to Limon. He said, *"I have never seen this happen before, especially out of Pueblo, but the judge just granted you emergency custody of the kids. You can go get them!"* Best news ever!

I thanked him, and as soon as I could, I turned around. I called my husband to tell him to turn around as well. We got a motel in Canon City so we could see our other daughter and fill her in on all the happenings. We had to wait on paperwork, but the next day we would head home with Amber's kids.

The next day we headed towards Colorado Springs. We had to give the lawyer time to get the paperwork and go in to sign everything. He would then fax everything back to the judge, and we could set up the Pueblo police to go get our kids. My husband and I went to have some breakfast, and wait on the ok to go to Pueblo. Perfect timing! We had just finished breakfast when our lawyer called and said, "we have a go!" We went and picked up copies of our emergency custody papers and headed to Pueblo.

With papers in hand, we entered the Pueblo Police Department. No one knew what we were up to. The Police did not know until we got there. The captain suspected, but he did not know until we showed up with the papers in hand. We were led by the captain to a conference room. Several others joined us during that conference. We told them our intentions were to have them pick up the kids and bring them to us at the station.

They agreed to do just that. They couldn't refuse us because the judge signed off on our papers. They told us about Amber's case. The captain explained how dangerous Amber's murderer was. He told us how he should have never been released, but the last case they had against him there was not enough evidence to keep him. He told us that they had way more evidence in Amber's case. Enough to keep him for life.

It was an emotional conference for my husband and I. We made it through it, and the police sent someone over to Amber's in laws to get our kids. They had no warning so they could not hide our kids from us. I heard that Amber's mother-in-law was furious that they didn't even know we were coming. That in its self was so incredibly gratifying for us. Before the police left to pick up our grandchildren, we told them that if Amber's 19-year-old daughter wanted to come home she was welcome to come with her siblings.

The police told her that we said she was an adult and could take care of herself. They told our granddaughter we did not want her! I was surprised that she didn't come with her siblings. When I asked the police, they told me she didn't want to come to us. Before Amber was murdered, my eldest granddaughter reported her mother missing. Our granddaughter reported her mother on May 17th. She called the police department every day to see if they were looking for her. That never happened either. Not according to the Police. According to the police department, Amber wasn't reported missing until her husband reported her the day before or the day she was discovered!

Why did the police lie to both of us? They claim they didn't! The lady investigator also thought it was necessary to tell me that the kids had to be put in school in Nebraska. Really! I didn't know that! Thanks for setting me straight on that. Like they didn't go to school their entire years with me. I am not impressed with Pueblo, the Police Department, the Courts, the Judges, The DA's office, or Victim Services! Had the police gone out and looked for Amber when her daughter reported her missing, she might still be alive! Oh wait! She didn't report her mother missing according to them! Her husband reported her missing and he was in jail. Conveniently enough, He reported her missing when it was too late to save her! How does that not scream, my husband set me up to be killed?

CHAPTER TWO
The Investigation

With Facebook notifications silenced, I was free to have a beep less day. My husband and I moved into our retirement house on the 20th of December, 2020. Our plans were to modernize our old 5-bedroom house and sell it to pad our retirement nest egg a bit. That never happened. Instead, we modernized our retirement house to sell it.

I suppose I thought if I did not acknowledge all the questions from Amber's friends and acquaintances, it could not be true and it would all blow over. Amber would get ahold of me and tell me how she was part of a big sting operation. They caught the bad guys and she was calling to tell me she was alright.

That did not happen either. Something similar happened before, but Amber just went missing for a while, she was not dead. I needed a hose connection for a garden hose, so I jumped in my car and drove to the Lexington Walmart to find what I needed. I did not want to be home alone.

On the way home from Walmart the New Mexico Investigators called me. First, the investigator wanted to know if my granddaughter spoke to me. I told him we spoke and she told me her mother, was dead. Then he wanted to know if I knew of anyone who might want to murder my daughter. I asked him if he was sure the person, he was talking about was my daughter. He verified that they were sure that the body they found was Amber. He also assured me that the information he gave me had not been released to the public yet.

My heart still stops when thinking about that day. It was the worse day ever! I asked if they had any idea who murdered my daughter, and who in their right mind would dump her along side a dirt road like she was yesterday's trash! I told the investigator about the gang Amber had been involved in while living in Nebraska.

I told him about the acquaintance that already knew Amber had died. I told him that her old friend was the first person to call me. I told him about Ambers current husband, and how I was sure that he had something to do with her murder. I poured my heart out to that investigator. He in turn passed everything over to the Pueblo Colorado Investigators. In all fairness he had to pass Amber's case to Pueblo.

At the time of Amber's death, she was a Pueblo resident. The New Mexico investigators along with the Pueblo Police Investigators, discovered that Amber had been shot at a business called The Wolfs Den in Pueblo. So, Amber died in Pueblo and her body was taken over 250 miles to be dumped in the Pecos New Mexico area.

Why did the Pueblo Investigating team not think it was important to investigate who the murderer called when he placed a call from his cell phone. He was sitting in his pickup at or on the railroad tracks.

Why would the murderer take Amber all the way to New Mexico to dump her body? Did Gonzales Ranch have anything to do with Amber?

Was that the killers dumping ground? He was accused of murder before Amber's death. Was he showing someone that he took care of her?

I found out how to order Amber's autopsy. I ordered that and waited. I needed the autopsy in order to be certain. Until I received the autopsy, my mind did not believe that Amber was not coming home to tell me anything, ever!

As soon as Pueblo Investigators took over Amber's case everything went downhill. They claimed to have questioned the current husband. They claimed to have asked him about his involvement with the man who murdered his wife. They claimed he did not "look" like he recognized the name when they told him who their suspect was. The Investigator told me that as the husband went into jail the murderer was going out of the jail. The investigator claimed that there was no way the two could have communicated. No way at all!

I found out from Amber's youngest daughter; she did meet the murderer before she saw him at the motel they were staying at. She met him at the first house they lived in while in Pueblo. Interesting that she spotted him leaving the husbands converted garage. Interesting that Amber's husbands mother owned that house. Interesting that she made them move from that house after they did so much work on it.

An investigator came to Nebraska to question Amber's children.

They did get that information from Amber's youngest daughter. Amber's youngest daughter also told the investigator that she saw the same man dealing drugs from the converted garage. Her big sister verified that drugs were being dealt out of what was supposed to be her apartment. Everything was reported to the investigators, they claimed they had enough evidence to put Amber's murderer away forever. That did not happen.

My family and I spent a lot of moments working through different scenarios. Every scenario led us back to the beginning of our huge circle of evidence. Amber's murderer knew her husband and contrary to the murderers' statement Amber knew him for some time before he killed her. She even went on a trip to Florida with her murderer and two other young ladies. Amber's mother-in-law was somehow involved. She most likely was only involved in the protecting her son aspect. Amber's husband had ties to the same gang Amber thought she broke free from in Nebraska.

Amber was no angel, but she was kind to those who needed kindness. She gave herself a bad name, because she did not care who she hurt. When Amber saw a wrong, she fixed it. No, she was not raised that way. She convinced herself that she needed to be that way to survive. Some people saw the best of Amber, others saw the worse. Anyone who could hurt a child, or a woman saw the worse. Anyone who stole from her or someone she knew, saw the bad side of Amber. Anyone who messed with her family, paid dearly. Amber saw many things that I never imagined she would see. The life she led made me cringe. I feared for her life on many occasions. Like when she would disappear for weeks at a time. If you feared my daughter, it was because you did something to be fearful of. Otherwise, Amber would do anything for anyone. She was also loyal to her friends, right up to when they messed her about.

Amber was not new to Police visits. She broke laws. She drove without a license; she took the law into her own hands. Run ins with the law was something Amber knew a lot about. Amber's lack of morals came from taking the drugs she took. She was remorseful when she was clean and did not give a damn when she was not clean. Her invincibility complex was another drug side effect. She could not stay in one place too long. I used to love going on shopping trips with Amber.

I stopped going when I could no longer keep up with her. Her mood changes, and accepting consequences did not exist when she was what I call strung out. I used to think that addiction was not an illness. The past few years has shown me otherwise. The beginning is a choice. Once you get in though, there is no coming out without a lot of hard work. Other people can't help you. Other people can guide you, and support your efforts. You have to clean yourself up.

I think that the police saw just another addict. I started a fundraiser for Amber's children and asked everyone involved with her case to share and help since they believed our family did not meet restitution requirements. They never responded! Oh, but they made sure to tell us how sorry they were for what our family went through, and I guess they saved us more money by not going to trial. By not going to trial they also showed us they did not give a damn. I also think that many in law enforcement see addicts as lost causes. You can't help them! They are beyond help! No!

You can help them if you provide services that get them off the drugs they are taking and make those services last a minimum of 3 years. You could make it based on how long a person has been using, but you will likely get repeat addicts that way. So, a new addict could take a year when a seasoned addict would need 2 or more years. Programs can be put into place that will actually help people addicted. Amber did not want to be an addict. She wanted to be understood. She wanted things to not be so hard. She wanted to be cared about, but the law did not care about her.

The law in Nebraska used Amber to catch bad guys. They used her for her connections. To be honest, I think Amber liked playing both sides. It was a thrill for her. The bad guys trusted her for a while. The Pueblo investigation team that worked on Amber's case did not give a damn about Amber. She was another addict off the streets that are literally littered with addicts. How many Ambers have to die this way? Again, why did the police wait to put out a missing persons report until Amber's husband reported her. Why on earth are they lying about my granddaughter reporting her mother missing? Did they mislead our family on purpose?

Amber was not important enough to the police for them to care that she was dead. They no longer had to "waste" man power on her. "She wasn't exactly a law-abiding citizen!" Your daughter hurt a lot of people herself, maybe this is karma!" These are the things I was not prepared to see. The Facebook comments about Amber boiled our family's blood. These things came from people who knew nothing about Amber. While we are on the topic of people bashing deceased people. Here is something to think about. Amber is a spirit now. Her murderer has an illness that he can not walk away from. He is going to die a slow painful death. Think about that!

There is an informant in the police department. That informant gave Amber's information to the media. How do I know this? When my eldest granddaughter told the media they were reporting information about her mother that was untrue and not released because of an ongoing investigation, that person told her they have an informant in the police department. Imagine losing your mother this way, and being told they can do what ever they want to. Total disregard to anyone else's rights to privacy.

The investigation led the police to Mr. Pearce. He turned on Amber's murderer. Despite the murderer threatening Mr. Pearce, and his wife, and several others Mr. Pearce told the police who killed Amber. Investigators did not send us any discovery letters. Pearce and the murder received each other discoveries, but we didn't get anything, and didn't know what was in the discoveries. After court I spoke with Pearce via jail mail. He told me almost everything that was in his discovery. His wife sent me the discovery letter. I read through it.

When I saw Mr. Pearce for the first time, I wanted to punch him. I wanted him to pay for Amber's death. Then I spoke to him. He begged me to listen. Something inside of me stirred. I stopped being angry and I listened. He told me that he did see my daughter that day. She walked into his establishment with her murderer. She leaned against the wall and spoke with him. The murderer got Amber involved in moving guns, and drugs for him. He told her the drugs and guns were his. Amber moved the guns and drugs. Pearce told her those guns and drugs were not his to move. She tried to get them back, but the people she sold them to sold them on to the next buyer.

Pearce left for 30 minutes or more to run errands, besides he didn't want to be there while the murderer was there. He did not like him. Amber was alive when he left. When he returned, he went to the kitchen. Pearce was in the kitchen when he heard the first gun shot. Amber was squatting against the wall. They were arguing. The murderer shot Amber. Shot Amber again then kicked her in the face and told her to die already, Bitch! The murderer had enough time to force Amber to take a cocktail of drugs. Her esophagus was coated with a powdery substance. The powdery substance in her esophagus was never tested. Why wasn't it tested?

That was the hardest thing I ever read. Why did the police not tell us about this? What kind of investigators are they? This was in Pearce's discovery. The murderer then threatened. Pearce. He made. Pearce put Amber in storage tote. Pearce told me that he never experienced anything like that. When he looked down at the tote, all he saw was Amber's eyes staring at him. This traumatic event gave him PTSD. Pearce was as much a victim as Amber was. I had to listen to him. I knew he was telling me the truth.

CHAPTER THREE
She Said Goodbye In So Many Ways!

Our grandchildren believe that their mom told them goodbye without telling them a proper goodbye. They believe that when she left on May 17th, 2021, she knew that she would not return. Amber spoke to her children about returning to Nebraska. She wanted a divorce because her husband did not turn out to be the man, she thought he was. Two weeks after she threatened him with divorce, she ended up dead.

Amber told her eldest daughter that she was going to sort out someone. I am sure that my daughter downsized her emotions for the sake of her children. She hugged them all and told them she would be back in a little bit. She left her eldest daughter 400 dollars and the room paid for a few days. Her actions tell me that she knew she was not coming back.

Amber also knew that I would do everything in my power to help her children. Some of the things she did before she died made us all question why she would treat her family like she did.

We have a theory as to why Amber talked crap about her family. She did not talk crap to our faces. The circumstances around Amber always put her in danger. Most of the time she had control of her situations. If the gangsters Amber chose to be around would have known about how close she was to her family, that would have put us all in danger. This theory came from way back when Amber first made her deal with the demons that controlled her.

Bad guys hang out in places that benefit them. They position themselves in high end jobs and approach people that they feel can help them. Young girls getting themselves mixed up with the wrong crowd make the best targets. *"Get them while they are young and make them the way you want them";* Amber once told me. If you could have heard the sadness in her voice. You would know. Amber came home early in the morning. She only had one child at that time, and that child was visiting her father.

Amber was visibly distraught. After I let her in, I sat down on the couch. She stood at the door, leaning against it a bit. The look on her face told me she needed to tell me something. I patted the couch for her to come sit down. When she walked in front of me, I noticed blood spattered on her shirt.

Her face was tear stained, and her eyes were red and puffy from crying. Her worry lines showed. I do not think she knew where to begin. I got up, went to the fridge and got her a cold Dr. Pepper. I hoped that would help ease her mind enough for her to talk to me. "Mom, you always seem to make me feel better, just being around." She spoke. I smiled softly at her. I asked her if she had been in a fight. She asked me why I thought she had been fighting. She fidgeted with the Dr. Pepper can in her hands. I took it from her and put it on the coffee table. She gave me a nervous smile and began talking.

"Mom, I witnessed a murder tonight. I'm sorry I came by so late, but I wasn't allowed to leave." I turned towards her on the couch so she could see I was paying attention and I cared about what she was telling me. My I'm listening face was on. Amber continued telling her story. "Mom, remember when I went to court the other day? I said "yes, I remember." "Well, when I told you to go out to the car, I would catch up to you, it was because someone wanted to talk to me." I said, ok. "Mom, they offered me a way to have everything I ever wanted, and all I have to do is follow their rules." Tonight, I had to see what happens when someone breaks the rules. Amber burst into tears! I scooted towards her and wrapped my arms around my young daughter. She cried uncontrollably for several minutes. Then she pushed away from me to continue her story.

"They made this girl who broke the rules get on her knees in front of me, mom. One guy pulled her head back by her hair so she had to look at me. Another man put a gun to her head and pulled the trigger, mom. It's her blood on my shirt." I pulled her back to me and let her cry until she was able to gain her composure again. "Mom, I don't know what to do," Amber sobbed. Still holding her, I told her she needed to get out of whatever she had gotten herself into. She needed to call the police.

She said "no, I can't do that mom. They have people in the police department. They have doctors, and lawyers, and even judges, mom. The only way out is to die, mom!" I didn't know what to say.

I just sat there holding my little girl who had got herself into something she didn't know how to get out of, and there was nothing I could do to fix it.

Amber's phone went off. She told me she had to go, but she would be back later. She gave me a smile, said, "don't tell anyone what I told you, mom," and out the door she went. I have never forgotten that talk.

When I found out Amber had been murdered, that conversation came back to me. The only way out for her was to die. Amber did not die without a fight. There were defensive wounds on her hands! I am pretty sure Amber fought her murderer while he was shoving drugs down her throat! Hence the defensive wounds on her fingers. Amber's autopsy proved that she was alive long enough for some of those drugs if not all of them, to get into her blood.

Amber would have overdosed if her murderer had not shot her twice. Based on Pearce's testimony to me, not to the court, Amber was not dyeing fast enough for her murderer. Hence the kick in the face, the Die already, Bitch, and the two shots to her chest that ended her life.

Amber did give the police the answers when they found the murdered girl's body. Amber helped the local police solve many murders, and she helped them take down a large number of drug dealers in the area we lived. The FBI offered Amber and her children protection, but Amber refused because the FBI told her they would not protect her parents.

Later down the road Amber asked me what I would do if we all had to disappear.

I did not know what I would do. I do know, I would have done anything to protect my daughter. Heck, I would do anything to protect all of my children.

In 2015 we moved away from the area where Amber got herself in so much trouble. She moved away as well. She went the opposite direction. Now I know why. Back then I did not even think about it. Along the way I thought about Amber's troubles, because they kept popping up. I guess that memory held on in the back of my mind. Amber's way of telling me goodbye? Maybe! Amber made sure to protect us by making sure that the demons in her life thought she didn't care about us. They only go after the ones you care about the most. So, she didn't show them she cared. She made up lies to make those demons think she hated us.

Amber's private conversations with us were totally Amber. Soft, full of love and her actions showed loyalty. Her way of protecting those she did love. Essentially, Amber bent over backwards, and gave up her life to protect her family. Even demons have codes they go by. One of those being; after the person you have a beef with is gone, you leave their family alone. Thankfully, no one has bothered us.

It may seem crazy, but I know my daughters spirit hangs around and helps us. Another one of her ways of showing us her love. I do not know who believes in spirits, but my family does. No, we are not crazy. Call it what you want, but the first sign of Amber being with me, was the rapid rain storm on highway 24 as I was trying to head home. The next sign of Amber was the storm that followed us home.

We got home and got the kids settled in. Darkness fell and lighting started. My grandson went out to the front porch to watch the storm. He saw his mother in the lightning. He came in and told me, "Her hair was lightening, and she had lightening streaks coming out her fingers, she had her arms stretched out. It was her body shape, grandma, and her eyes were glowing, she looked awesome, and so powerful! It was really mom; do you believe me. "Yes, I do believe you, and I wish I had seen her too." I hugged my grandson, and we sat together on the front porch for a long time. Each of us in our own thoughts. Probably about his mother.

The wind kicked up, and I said, "Amber, you better not break my flower pots this time." Well, the storm moved through quickly. My grandson and I went out to enjoy the night air, and check on the flower pots. Not a single pot was broken. Several were knocked over, but the plants and the pots were in better-than-expected condition. There is a joke about that, at our house. When Amber got mad, she threw things. Things like plant pots with baby plants in them.

There was another storm in Pueblo, that same night. Before I tell you about the storm, I need to tell you how my daughters mother-in-law treated her. This will not make sense unless I show you.

Amber's mother-in-law did not like her son marrying a white girl. She wanted her son to be with his Mexican ex who was worse than Amber in so many ways. She did have a son with the woman so, I guess that could be why she wanted that. The mother-in-law treated Amber like she was beneath her family. She was never going to be good enough for her family. It did not matter what Amber did. Amber wanted to be accepted. She was led to believe that the family she married into was all about family. They were not.

The mother-in-law used Amber as her maid, and personal errand runner. Amber was happy to please her until she had only negative things to say about her. Eventually, Amber got tired of being treated like a maid, personal errand runner. She cried to her eldest daughter and told her that she was done trying to please the mother-in-law.

She stayed away from her for 3 or 4 months. The mother-in-law, not used to doing her own house cleaning and running her own errands, came to see Amber. She made up to her and managed getting back in Amber's good books. Everything went well until Amber let her guard down. The mother-in-law reverted to using my daughter, talking crap about her, and talking down to her. That is not all the she did.

When Amber was murdered her husband automatically became her heir. Amber's husband was in jail though. He signed my daughter over to his mother. I think he did that to stop me from having an autopsy done in Nebraska. I would have done that. The husbands mother cremated my daughter.

She possibly did that to hide any involvement in her murder. Wait, there's more! As if our family had not been through enough, Amber's in laws cost us over 28 thousand dollars in legal fees when all they had to do was call me to come get my grandchildren.

It was not enough that Amber died, that family started talking crap all over social media as well. The husband got out of jail in December and ended up giving my eldest granddaughter her mother's ashes. Her ashes are home in Nebraska where she is loved and truly missed.

Back to that storm. The one that happened in Pueblo on the same night we had a big storm in Nebraska. Brace yourself. It is a storm! Amber's hoity toity mother-in-law got her expensive pots broke up, and 9 out of 12 of her marijuana plants broken beyond repair. Not only that but Amber's mother-in-law passed away just under 12 months after Amber did. Our family came back together after Amber's murder. Her hoity toity mother in laws family broke up and they all scattered. Each blamed the other for their mother's death.

The funny thing about spirits is that they are real. They do not like it when their families are mistreated. They try to right wrongs. I can give many more examples. Like, when Amber's daddy went to Walmart to look for string for her memorial garden and the green string fell off the shelf and landed by his feet. (Her favorite color)

Then there are the drug busts of people Amber knew and didn't like because they sold drugs to children. I believe that Amber wanted me stop and listen to Pearce.

She wanted me to blame the right person for her death. The moral of the above stories is this: Don't judge people by what you hear, or read. If you can not look deeper, stop looking at them. You do not know their story unless you know them. If you go around being heartless, and putting people down Karma won't get you. God will.

We never know when our time is up. Amber did not ask to be murdered. Our family did not ask for this incredible pain, but we are not alone. People lose their loved ones daily. When you lose someone without being there for them, it deepens that grief. We never dreamed of this.

Amber and I used to have deep discussions. I told her when I go, I will come back and tell you what it's like. She told me the same. I woke up earlier than usual one morning. The smell of coffee woke me up. I went downstairs. Amber was making me coffee. Her eldest daughter was talking to her. She smiled at me and held out her hand. Are you ready momma? I took her hand and she flew me right through the walls of our home. Up past the clouds. She flew me though the universe. Then I woke up in my bed. There was no coffee. I had to make my own.

CHAPTER FOUR
It's Judicial

Amber had many dealings with the judicial system. Her first dealing with court was when she forged one of her adopted grandfathers' checks. Amber was sentenced to a year in the Nebraska Women's Prison in York Nebraska. It was a stupid thing to do, and I could not believe she stole from the only grandfather she ever knew. That one stupid moment set the stage for the rest of Amber's life, and I told her that.

Amber made a lot of stupid decisions throughout her life, but that was the one that stopped her from going to college, and getting good work. She could not even get a passport anymore. Felons do not get to have rights that others get. Once you are labeled a felon you are a felon for life. So, boys and girls, do not make yourself a felon. It is not worth it!

Amber could not change becoming a felon, but she could have made her life better. She was an incredibly smart, beautiful young lady with so much potential. She should have created a business of her own. Something legit that is. Instead, Amber stuck to the destructive path she was on. No matter how many times I told her she was making things harder for herself, she kept making things harder.

When she got out of prison in Nebraska, she attempted going to college for criminal justice. That lasted a few months.

She never kept her drivers license up to date which kept getting her into more trouble. Driving without a license is illegal, as is driving without insurance on your vehicle. When Amber stopped even attempting to do the right thing, we stopped allowing her to use our cars. *Since you won't get your license; you are not going to drive our cars.* Amber began getting into other trouble. Trouble that landed her in substance abuse court. She went to drug court which was supposed to help. How is it helpful to make people go through a program that they have to pay thousands of dollars to go through? The program in question is suppose to teach the criminals how to take accountability for their actions, by teaching them that they are doing wrong. Addicts are to join AA and NA as part of the program.

When a person gets court ordered to go through the program if they can not afford it, they get put back in jail or prison to finish their sentence. The court is setting these people who are already down, up to fail. It's a legalized money-making scheme. The courts profit by putting these people through their program. I told Amber to do her time, because they were wasting her time, and not at all helping her.

Amber was trying to work a minimum wage job, sometimes two jobs, pay for her court class, and probation fees, her rent, her utilities, and gas in her car.

It is overwhelming to think of all the hoops they had my daughter jumping through. It did not benefit her; it only benefited the courts pocketbook. There must be a better way. With all the million, and billionaires in the world, why can't someone start a program that helps people instead of setting them up for failure?

People's minds are extremely versatile. We can put ourselves through so much and still bounce back. Amber was proof of that. People can be hand picked to be trained to do better if someone is willing to use patience and understanding to do it. The program cannot be government funded. It has to be funded by the private sector. There cannot be any way that clients can get ahold of drugs of any sort. Two years before she was murdered, Amber wanted to start a program that would help people like her. She told me her plans. Those plans were amazing. She could have helped so many.

I agree that some people are past the helping stage, but my

daughter was not one of those people.

Why does the judicial system blame the victims? In Amber's case, her murderer told the court that Amber stole drugs from the Cartel. He said he had to kill her. His lawyer claimed that his client was remorseful because he said she shot Amber twice in the chest. Amber did not steal the anything.

Her killer stole guns then had Amber sell them. That's not remorse! Amber's killer did not confess to all he did to her. If he was remorseful, he would have told us that he stuffed drugs down Amber's throat in the hopes she would die.

He would have said that she wasn't dying fast enough for him so he kicked her in the face then shot her twice in the chest. What Amber's killer did was defamation of Amber's character. He purposely made her look bad to get a deal for himself.

Pearce's discovery statement said that the murderer told Amber the drugs and guns were his and her killer wanted her to help move them. Amber clearly was the victim! Yes, she should not have gotten herself involved in the mess she was in. Still, her murderer did not deserve any sort of plea deal. It's not Judicial to blame victims! It's not Judicial to give a murderer 42 years when his victim received the death sentence. Amber did stupid things, but none of what she did ever in her life was worth her having to die!

The Judicial system could do away with a lot of prison over crowding if they would go back to their kill and be killed mind set. Amber did not receive Justice from the court! The court let her down one last time. They clearly had the mindset that Amber got what she deserved, even though they said, "No one deserves to die like this." The Judges actions and sentence was a clear slap in the face to Amber, her children, and her parents.

The DA's office takes cases like Amber's case and they shove it under the rug. It's cost money to hold trials. So, let's just offer plea deals instead of punishing murderers. I reached out to the DA's office when Pearce was getting ready for court.

The following was the response I received along with my reply.

Carol,

Our cases are often resolved on the evidence we have available to us and the cooperation of witnesses. There is often a difference between moral guilt and punishment and legal justice. Legal justice is not always what we'd like to have happen in a case, but what is consistent with the evidence available. We also coordinate with the victims in the case so they understand what we are doing. They don't always agree, but at least we have explained the case and our limitations or restrictions.

I appreciate your input, but we proceed with a case given the best information we have available to us.

R/Jeff

No! No, you do not! You offered Amber's killer 42 years for being a good boy and confessing to shooting Amber twice. He did not just shoot Amber twice! He tortured her for 3 to 4 days and dumped drugs and alcohol down her throat. The evidence is in her autopsy report, which I have read! The evidence was never allowed the light of day. So, don't lie to me. There is nothing I despise worse than people who lie to me.

Also how dare you! Do not treat me, Amber's mother, like I am some sort of idiot! There were loads of evidence, and it's not too late to back out of Pearce's deal! They held her at his place of business and then her murderer killed her.

Thank you for the evidence to which I will use against your office!

Have a great new year!

I spoke with Mr. Pearce afterwards. So, I did not have knowledge of his findings report at the time. The DA's office response to me provoked me to contacting Mr. Pearce through jail mail. Our family got a lot of closure reading through Pearce's discovery letter. In the above reply from the DA's office, Jeff states that their cases are often resolved on the evidence they have available to them and the cooperation of witnesses. That is a downright lie. There was a ton of evidence and several witnesses who were never allowed to speak because the DA's office offered a deal to Amber's killer. It will always be the good boy deal to me!

There is often a difference between moral guilt and punishment and legal justice. This was a load of crap talk. Did he think that through?

Legal justice is not always what we'd like to have happen in a case, but what is consistent with the evidence available. The evidence available was not introduced in a trial, because there was never a trial. The court did hear the evidence and there was a lot of evidence. I laid in my bed with covid listening to 4 hours of evidence. Amber's autopsy report was never offered into evidence. Why?

We also coordinate with the victims in the case so they understand what we are doing. Really? When did you coordinate with Amber's eldest daughter? How about never! Your office never spoke to Amber's eldest daughter. Your office never spoke to Amber's youngest children. You did not coordinate with anyone except me. The DA's office flat lied to me. They manipulated me into accepting a plea deal by telling me that Amber's killer got into a fight and something that they could not tell me happened. They could only tell me that they knew whatever happened would bring our family closure. *It would make me happy!*

What happened was Amber's killer got into a fight while in jail. During that fight, he confessed to shooting Amber twice in her chest. Wow! The DA's office twisted that in their favor. Let's just trick the victim's family into allowing us to offer a plea deal. Trials are costly, the more we can push through the more our voters will love the fact that we saved our city money. Yaaaaay, go us!

They don't always agree, but at least we have explained the case and our limitations or restrictions.

Wow, again! They did not explain anything. They did not have limitations, or restrictions. They did not have to offer Amber's killer a plea deal to tell us, her family, that he shot Amber twice in the chest. Again, the evidence was overwhelming, and they had many witnesses. So, really, based on Jeff's straight forward message to me, the city of Pueblo has a devious DA who will make up excuses as to why a multi murderer can make it back on the streets in 42 years. I'm so happy I do not live in Pueblo!

I appreciate your input, but we proceed with a case given the best information we have available to us.

Why, Thank you from the bottom of Amber's family's ice-cold hearts. We sure do appreciate the hard work you did not do. I bet Amber appreciates your severe lack of concern over her, as well. Good Job helping us get Justice for Amber!

Now let's talk about restitution!

The Judge ordered restitution to be paid by Amber's killer to her family. I sent in the request for restitution but the DA's office denied restitution. Each time I was denied by phoned. I was phoned so that there is no record of what they told me. Even though the judge ordered restitution to be paid, our family will receive nothing. We were told that because of the circumstances of Amber's death we are not eligible. We were told via phone conversation, so I can not show evidence of those conversations, but I was called twice.

It would have been nice to have a little help, as my husband and I had the costs of motels, travel from and back to Nebraska, plus the lawyer fees for having to fight for our grandchildren. Had the killer not killed Amber we would not have had anything to pay. Amber would have brought her children to us if she needed to. Amber's youngest would not have had to go to counseling. We would not have had to pay for braces for her son. It will be a long time before we can retire, because Amber was murdered and we need to finish raising our grandchildren. The Colorado Judicial System did not care. The DA's office saved Pueblo a ton of money by refusing our restitution. It is alright. We will be ok. More importantly, Amber's children will be perfectly fine.

Mr. Pearce's' Discovery statement

I mentioned that the accused accomplice and I spoke after I emailed the DA's office. I was looking for answers, and I received what I was looking for. The below is that conversation. I instigated the conversation. At first, I did not believe Mr. Pearce. I thought he was just telling me what he thought I wanted to hear. I read and re read his words. I feel like Amber wanted me to blame the right person. Mr. Pearce isn't exactly a model citizen, but I do believe him. He did not hurt Amber.

> *Me:*
>
> *Hello Mr. Pearce*
> *This is Amber's mother. Now that court is finished, I have every right to confront you over your court statements. You can deny, deny, deny, but we, Amber's family, know that you lied! Omitting is lies!*
>
> *We know Amber was tortured. Her autopsy tells the actual truth. We know Amber went missing on the 17th of May! We know why Amber was murdered and we know you had more to do with her death! You may have fooled the DAs office, but we knew Amber, and you didn't fool her family!*
>
> *You have PTSD over Amber because she knows the truth too! I know you are Native. I have Native in me, but my Native is still connected. I know your nightmares are from Amber! She will torture your mind like you and Roy tortured her. Spirits can't lie! You know they can't.*
>
> *What you didn't know is that Amber's Native son dreamt about her death before he found out she was dead! You didn't know that I felt her dying! The part you played in Amber's death will haunt you for the rest of your life, because you didn't come clean.*

There may be some truth in your words, and I know if you told all the truth, you would be dead as well. Self-preservation is real. This will be the only message I will send you aside from Amber's story. I will send her book to you after I release it on the second anniversary of her murder. I will also pray for your soul! I forgive you, Sean Pearce! Can you forgive yourself?
Sincerely
Carol Staff
Amber's momma

Sean:

Mrs. Staff,
I understand that you and your family will blame and hate me forever for what you believe about my involvement in your daughter's death and no matter what I tell you or how many times it has been said you will continue to hate me and continue to not believe me because of what you believe happened. I do however care very very much about how you and your Family feel and knowing the truth about what happened that night is also very important to me. I was and continue to be totally honest about the events that occurred that night and told the complete and honest truth from the very beginning and will continue to tell you the truth.

I assure you Mrs. Staff, Amber was never tortured the night Roy killed her and as far as I knew Amber chose to be with Roy and I truly had only met her once before and her and I had spoken about her making some signs for the clubhouse and she had about 20 titles from various farm vehicles and equipment that she was trying to sell. I truly have no reason whatsoever to lie to you about the events of that night and please believe me I sincerely empathize with your family about your loss.

I have never liked or associated with Roy and all of this started because I had called him a retard told him that I didn't want him hanging around my business or my home so he decided to break in and steal a bunch of items and had your daughter sell them for him. Well, when the true owners contacted Roy and told him it was their items he had stolen and he Had better get it all back. They came to the clubhouse that night and got 2500 dollars from me to supposedly go and retrieve the stolen property.

They were gone for a while before they returned and were arguing and calling each other names and Amber said that she couldn't get the property back because the people she had sold it to wanted drugs and not money for the property. I had my back to them doing the day's receipts and doing the books when Roy shot Amber the first time. I swear to you on my life that as soon as I turned around and saw what had happened, I tried to get in between them and help your daughter, I then seen blood on her chest and knew that he had shot her. Roy then stepped in between Amber and I and tried to hit me with the pistol, and went up to Amber and shot her again. It was the worst thing in my life that I have ever witnessed and I assure you that your daughter WAS NOT tortured, she died immediately after that asshole shot her the second time.

Yes, I sometimes still have dreams of what happened that night but believe me it's not a haunting, it's always Amber reaching out to me to help her. I did everything I could do to help her and she knows it. I too was supposed to die that night and I know that if Roy could have gotten us both in that truck, I would be dead now too. I know that are going to continue to hate me and not believe a word I have to tell you but I do hope that the spirits have some way to show you that I am telling you the truth and not

Me:

Sean, I know you can't tell me the truth. I know that sections of what you tell me are true. Amber had 16 different drugs in her tox report. Her esophagus was coated in a foreign powder! That is drugs dumped down her throat while she was lying in a flat position. Amber's face was Swollen and bruised! You can't bruise after your dead because your blood is no longer circulating through your body. Amber's face was unrecognizable! I did order the crime scene photos. I saw my daughter. I believe the proof. The images my daughter showed me before the police showed up to tell me my daughter was dead and before I saw who killed her was your face with sad eyes and a gentle smile. I know you feel remorse because of the image Amber sent me. I then saw Roy with crazy scary eyes and contempt all over his face. So, I do understand and the spirits are talking to me. Amber was cremated. She is back home! As I said! I forgive you. You need to speak to Amber for your forgiveness from her. She's listening!

Sean:

I am not omitting anything, every investigator, Attorney and prosecutor knows that I told the truth and did everything I could to make sure that piece of shit spends the rest of his life in prison and as I said in court the only thing, I regret is being afraid for my own life and not going to the police sooner than I did. Roy was going around looking for me telling people, even my landlord that he was going to kill me as soon as he found me. Does that sound to you like we were in cahoots together?

I've been jumped 3 times now and had the shit kicked out

of me for doing the right thing and telling the truth and now I have to do the rest of this sentence knowing this is probably going to happen quite often because I am now considered a rat and an informant because I did the right thing for your daughter. I thank you for your forgiveness and I know in my soul that Amber holds nothing against me because she does know I tried to stop what happened that night. I can't say that it doesn't truly bother me that you and your family will forever hate and blame me and will not accept the truth from me about what happened but believe me I wanted nothing more but to go to trial and PROVE my innocence to your family but when I found out that I would have to take the stand to defend myself and that my past criminal history would defy any truth I was to tell , my attorney advised me it would in best interests to accept the offer, that is what I chose to do.

I will never run or hide from the truth or your Family and I will always address you or anyone who wishes to talk to me about what happened. I know you probably don't want to accept a lot of what I tell you or have to say about what truly happened because it won't be congruent with your book, but I assure you, once again, that I have nothing to gain or lose by my honesty to you. I completely sympathize with you and your family for your loss and you are right, it will be in my memories for the rest of my life, but not because of the part you believe I played in Amber's death but because I couldn't stop it from happening. If you can ever get past your hatred and blame of me, I will always be happy to speak with you whenever you would like.

Me:

I have no hatred for you. I can't say the same for Roy! So much for the first message being the last. I don't know about how much blame I put on you. I do know that Roy carries most the blame as I have dreams about how he is faring. Tell me everything. I can take it.

Sean:

Thank you and I can assure you that I am a good person and NOT the animal that it would take to do the horrible things that you have blamed me of doing. Yes, I have an extensive past criminal history but all of my cases are drug related or criminal impersonation. (Giving the cops a fake name) I can put you in touch with several accountable people who will more than vouch for my character. My secretary, my wife, my family will all attest that I am NOT a bad or evil person. I was doing great, the best I have ever done in my life, I had everything I ever wanted and my business was legal. That worthlessness piece of shit turned my whole world upside-down and has been my enemy for many years. He is the one and only person I truly hate and because of his fame from the A&E show (LOCKDOWN) he is idolized by all the other pieces of shit in prison and I truly don't know if I will even make it through this sentence alive either. If I don't I have no doubts in my mind that Amber will greet me as a friend as she did when she was alive.

Me:

I don't want accreditation of your character. I want to know why my daughter's face was unrecognizable. She didn't get those bruises from a ride to New Mexico, as her body was no longer able to bruise. She was dead! I want to know how Amber could be standing with 16 different drugs in her body washed down with alcohol. All of that was introduced to her blood stream at least 30 mins before her heart stopped pumping! You understand now why I don't believe? The fentanyl alone would have killed her. So, Sean, if it wasn't you who was it?

Me:

By the way.... I am a good person. Good people don't sell drugs! Good people don't traffic drugs. Good people don't deserve losing their child like this. Amber was a naughty girl too! I know my daughter. Everything that led Amber to her death will be in her book. All her story.

Sean:

I'm not sure of how much of the Discovery you were able to access but I got to listen to your recordings with the investigators and heard you yourself attest to Ambers Parenting and lifetime drug use. I heard all about Amber's husband and her pending settlement and your beliefs about a conspiracy involving all that. I assure you I know nothing about Amber's drug use because I am not a drug dealer, I was a drug supplier and only picked up and delivered large amounts of meth only to other dealers throughout the state, I never dealt drugs on a street level.

As to Ambers body's state, After Roy and Amber came and picked up the money to go and attempt to retrieve the property they left, Roy came in and got the money from me and Amber stayed in the truck on the phone Roy said. (?) They returned approximately a half hour later arguing and told me that Amber couldn't get the items back because they wanted drugs not money. I assure you Amber was quite Mobil and vocal in her argument with Roy. When they came into my office Amber immediately walked behind me and said " Hey, what's up" and then went and squatted down on her knees against the wall in the office as there was only one chair in the office.

I continued to do my receipts while they argued about Amber not being able to get the property back and that there was some of the 2500 missing. Their argument became more intense and I heard Amber say that Roy had called her a rat and Amber then yelled at him that she had tried to get the Stuff back and couldn't because they wanted drugs not money. That's when the first gunshot went off! It scared the living shit out of me and I immediately turned around and saw Amber looking at her hand that she had obviously touched to her chest to see if she had indeed been shot.

That's when I yelled " Hey, what the fuck" and got in between Amber and Roy. Roy took a swing at me with the pistol and went up to her and put the gun against her chest at an angle towards her heart and pulled the trigger again. He then kicked her in the face and said " hurry up and die bitch" then he went over to the big tub I had old cloths in and dumped the cloths out and said "help me get her in this" by this time

I assure you Amber was dead and no longer breathing. Roy then ordered me at gunpoint to help him put her in the truck or I was going to die too. It hurt so bad to see her face looking at me that I took the trash bag and covered the bin. After I helped Roy put Amber in the truck, I immediately started my bike and left my business open, went home and told my wife everything that had happened. All of this is in the discovery that I will be more than glad to let you read.

I told the truth from the beginning and I'm telling you the truth right now. Not only was I truthful but the investigators picked up my wife for questioning four hours before they came and got me and I informed my wife to be completely honest also. From the whole time of Roy and Amber showing back up to the clubhouse to Me leaving on my bike was probably a half hour.

Me:

Thank you!

I didn't get any discovery at all. I have been left with nothing but a whole lot of pain, and Amber's kids. I'm the one fixing Amber's mistakes. No matter what we have been through with Amber, she did not deserve to die like this.

Sean:

Sorry about not getting back with you until now, we have tablet blackout time from 2:30 till 4:30 where we cannot use the tablets. I will speak with my wife about sending you all the discovery concerning this case because I want you and your family to see and understand that I have been honest from the beginning and also did what I could to be the one and only eye witness to what happened that night. No, Amber did not deserve what happened to her that night and PLEASE, PLEASE, PLEASE believe me

I do feel your pain and loss! I too have a daughter about the same age as Amber who is a drug addict and alcoholic who chooses to love a man who has beaten her, broke her arm and one of her legs, and has been charged with domestic violence over seven times and she swears she loves him. She blames me for every single thing wrong in her life even though I have never ever even raised a hand to her. I had one domestic violence charge when I was in my 20s so she can't even say that it was a learned behavior of how she grew up but I know in my heart that this man is going to be the death of her. She has already lost her children and lives with her mom whom is at her wits end with her too. I will get back with you about sending you the discovery as soon as I discuss it with my wife.

Me:

Sean, I speak to you from experience now. Let your time with my Amber teach you to never give up on your daughter! Amber blamed me for anything and everything that went wrong in her life. Reality is, I never have been an addict myself. I drink once or twice a year and only one small glass. The fact is that I bent over backwards for Amber and I have cared for her children for a lot of years. Amber has had men in her life and each one hurt her more.

Me:

Sean, don't give up on your daughter. Take care! Our family forgives you! Stay safe in there. You should get out of that drug life!

Sean:

I truly appreciate your advice and believe me I will fallow it completely; I also thank you for your concern and mostly for your forgiveness, words cannot ever explain how truly thankful I am for your forgiveness. I spoke with my wife and she is in complete agreement that you should be able to read the discovery and she will gladly send it to you however you wish to receive it. Just simply let us know how or where you want it sent. I can tell you are an amazing human and I will forever regret the actions and circumstances that cost your daughter's life.

I will always remain at your disposal with whatever help I may give you; you only have to ask. My only request is that you please express my honest, heartfelt condolences for their loss. I'm not sure who feels how about what happened or if Amber's husband could possibly be seeking revenge against my wife and I worry constantly about her safety. I assure you she is also very Innocent in this situation and is more than willing to help out in any way she can. She IS a good person and is only involved in this because I confided completely in her from the night this happened until now.

Me:

I live in Nebraska. Your wife has never been in any danger from my family. Amber's husband is downright a bad guy. However, He didn't love Amber at all. He beat Amber's children with belts, smoked meth sitting beside my 11-year-old grandson, and asked my 11-year grandson permission to smoke next to him. Amber threatened to divorce him the week before she died. Roy got out when her husband went in. If her husband is trying to hurt your wife, it isn't because he cared about Amber.

Me:

It's because he is a lame brain idiot. He never cared for Amber. They married each other so they didn't have to go against each other in court. It's unbelievable how much I didn't know about my daughter. If your wife feels like she's in danger it probably has something to do with maybe Amber's husband is trying to take yours because in his stupid head you took his. He isn't very smart.

Sean:

Thank you for your clarification on that matter and once again thank you for hearing me out and granting me your forgiveness. If you want the discovery, send my wife Lynette a friend request and she will continue to help you in whichever way we can. I pray that the great spirit helps heal your hearts and shows you in every sunset the love and beauty your daughter left behind. Please feel free to contact me any time you need to.

Me:

Let me know if your Amber dreams stopped. She understands why you couldn't save her.

Sean:

Thank you, Carol, nothing has made me feel better since this whole thing happened than you and your families understanding and forgiveness.

Me:

I sincerely hope that Amber helps you make it through this.

Sean:

I've definitely had someone looking out for me!
Believe me sweet lady, this has been the lesson of my lifetime. Lynette and I are moving when I get out and I will NEVER have another Facebook account.

Me:

Great plan!

Sean:

You know a lot of untrue and horrible things have been said and printed about me, I do realize that I put myself in a lot of those situations by my actions that I now have to pay for. I understand the workings of drug addled minds and see that you too have suffered the slings and stones of your daughter blaming you for everything that has went wrong in her life as my daughter has me. I hate to impose on you but I would like to ask if there is any way that you could possibility help save the life of my daughter. she is so full of blame and hate and has given my wife much stress and strain for staying with me because she truly believes all the propaganda that has been circulated about me since this all transpired. Any word from you just may help immensely. I'm not asking you to speak to her personally because it would never do any good as she is so full of hatred, but maybe just a post that she is sure to see would me try to start mending her heart. Prior to you contacting me I had decided to cut her out of me and my wife's life but your text helped me to decide to never give up. Any help at all would be greatly appreciated Carol.

Me:

I'm working on it

You're amazing and probably more of a lifesaver than I proved to be... Thank you so much... Just know that Brandi has made up horrible stories about her upbringing. But I assure you Carol I have never raised a hand or abused any of my children, not even a swat on the diaper, EVER! I was abused as a child and I chose to break the cycle and never make my children have to experience what I had to go through growing up. Once again thank you so, so, much.

CHAPTER FIVE
More Than A Decade

No one knows more than the families of those effected by addiction what it is like to live the lifestyle. Amber checked herself into rehab and she checked herself out of rehab at least twice. Addiction is a daily struggle. Once you become an addict, you are an addict for life. This means that the craving is always there even if you are not using any more. No one is immune. All it takes is trying something to become addicted to it. The addict becomes addicted to the feeling.

They literally crave how their drug of choice makes them feel. They feel remorse for the things they do while on the drugs. They don't care when they are high. Their souls care! You can change your brain, but your soul struggles for control. Your soul tries to survive. The remorse you feel is your soul telling you to feel bad about what you did. If you do not feel bad for what you did, your soul is no longer good.

Addiction is a family thing. You are not alone. What you are addicted to makes you feel like you are alone. The drug you chose to do makes you paranoid. Drugs chemically changes how your brain works. So, when you think you are still the same, you are not! All you have to do is google meth addict image memes. People see you.

They make fun of how you are acting. How you act disgusts them. They will use your picture to get their point out and they will video you. You really do not want that, but you are too high to know they are seeing you. Addicts steal things to buy drugs. They steal from their family, friends, acquaintances, and stores. Addicts will even sell their government food stamp money to get money to buy their drugs.

Addicts do not just steal. They make up elaborate, believable stories to manipulate their way through life. For instance: One time, after Amber got paid from work, she called in the next day claiming that her daughter had been in a horrible accident and was at the hospital. Her boss called me, but I just took her daughter to school. Amber got so mad at me for not lying for her. She got fired from that job.

I realize what I write makes my daughter look bad. She was not a bad person. Her mind was riddled with grief over the things she did, and years of drug use. The point to take away from reading about our experiences is the power of the drugs addict's use. The drug has to power to short term cover your pain if you are an addict. It does not take your pain away.

The sores you get all over your body is caused by the drugs. Those chemicals are not supposed to be in your body. So, your body releases it in sores. For families dealing with addiction, look for those sores. You will Not need to look closely. Drugs have the power to take your child, your husband, your niece, your nephew, anyone you care about. You are powerless. It is up to the person who is using the drug, to stop using the drug, but you can continue to guide them and support them. Do not give them money.

Bad people take advantage of those addicted to drugs. Amber was approached by one of those bad people after one of her court dates. He had the power to make her court troubles go away. All she had to do was work for him. That is not all she had to do though. Those kinds of people don't care about you. Mr. Pearce said so himself. He worked for that sort of person. The only thing those kinds of people care about is lining their own pockets, and they all answer to someone higher than them. They are out there everywhere. As Amber said, "They are doctors, lawyers, judges, police officers, they position themselves in prominent positions. They offer you everything, but give you nothing. If it's too good to be true, it isn't real!

For more than a decade, Amber did "jobs" for the man that approached her after court. He did not give her the great life that he promised her. She tried to get me involved one time. All I had to do was drive from a pick-up point to a drop off point. "You will make 10 thousand dollars every trip momma". I told her I was not at all interested.

Amber told me that the risk involved would be very low for me, because of my age. I told Amber, the money sounded good, but the money was not worth it to me. I told her she needed to get away from those people. She smiled at me and said, "It's ok momma". She never mentioned it to me again.

I hoped that eventually, Amber would see how her choices affected her family, and be able to get away from the gang involvement. I thought she found a way. There was a large "bust" in the town we lived at. Amber disappeared for several weeks. Her dad and I thought she went to jail with everyone who had their name listed in the news paper, but Amber wasn't in jail. When she came home, she told me that she had been in jail for a few hours, but the FBI talked to her, and she was let out. She had valuable information for them, and they used that information and let her go. I do not know where she was for weeks. Amber did not elaborate.

Once in, "The only way out is death!" Amber tried to get away. She left her children with me for four years. She thought she got away, but her new husband was from the same gang she left many years before. She did not know until after she was married to him. When she met him, he held a gun to her head then claimed he thought she was someone else.

Things Amber said made us believe that she was forced to marry him or die. A get back in or you will die offer, so to speak. We believe that Ambers husband recognized her and was told to get her back in the fold or kill her. So, he gave her the marriage offer. When Amber told him she wanted a divorce, He had her killed. Why do we think he did that? The month before her murder, Amber's husband was arrested for stealing a pickup. The pickup he stole belonged to a man who gave little girls drugs in exchange for sex.

Amber knew one of the little girls the man was doing this to. Amber and her husband went to the man's house and Amber's husband stole the pickup. Amber's husband did the time for that crime, but he called me from jail after her death and angrily told me that he was in jail because of Amber. The husbands phone call was not used in the investigation, and there was no trial. Anger is motive, and because the killer and her husband knew each other that should have been suspicious, but the investigators did not see it like we did. So, they refused to look into that any further. The investigators had their killer. They did their job. They were not going to look any further into Amber's case. As far as they were concerned, the case was closed.

The Pueblo investigators told me when Amber's husband went into jail her murderer was being let out. Literally at the same time. Amber's husband knew her murderer but played it off to the investigators that he did not. Her husband was as much of an addict as she was, if not more so. Amber's husband introduced her to her murder before they were even married.

CHAPTER SIX
Amber's Murderer!

Amber's murderer killed at least two, maybe three times before killing Amber. We heard that from the Police Captain during our visit after Amber's death. They never had enough evidence against him to keep him in prison. The captain insisted that they had enough evidence this time. He told us Mr. Pearce turned on Amber's killer, but he did not tell us what Pearce said. We did not know about the discovery letters at all until Mr. Pearce told me via email.

Amber's killer had a twin brother. The twins had an extensive criminal background. They should be considered harden criminals. Because of television shows such as Lockdown, this type of criminal is instead idolized. People talk like they are good guys. No, they are terrible people, one of them killed a mother of 5. Her killer took her life so he did not get into trouble.

He blamed Amber for something she did because he convinced her, and lied to her. No, she should not have associated herself with someone like him. I know Amber, and I am sure that she helped him because he promised her a win fall from the proceeds of what he stole from Mr. Pearce's place of business. Was that how he set her up? I will never know, because I will never speak to him. Oh, I do want to, but I know it will do me no good.

The First Attempt On Amber's Life

Amber needed a tire for her car. She asked her husband for advice on where to get her tire fixed. She wanted somewhere that wasn't going to cost her a small fortune. Her husband sent her to a guy that did change her tire. The husband told Amber to just take the car over there and leave. The guy that was supposed to just change her tire rigged Amber's car so that the doors locked her in the car. When she showed up to check on her car, the hood was up. Since when do you need the hood up to change a tire? The guy that fixed her tire told Amber that he was checking the oil.

When Amber was about a block from the hotel her car was smoking. When she parked in the hotel parking lot her car was on fire. Her car doors would not unlock. Thank God, Amber had super strong legs. She kicked her way out of her burning car. Amber called her husband to tell him what happened. He was furious with her that she went to check on her car.

He accused her of staying there and messing around on him. He did not ask her if she was ok. Tell me again, why Amber's husband was not a prime suspect! She yelled at her husband, and told him never mind. She hung up the phone and took her other car to the guy's house. She went down the alley to the back yard. Amber got out of the car real fast. The guy had a look of shock on his face. Amber's eldest daughter witnessed the entire scene.

I imagine it was the deer in the headlight look. He looked Amber up and down, and repeatedly said he didn't do anything to her car. Amber did not believe him, but she left.

I told the investigation team about the car fire, and her husband's involvement. We believe that was her husband's first attempt at killing Amber, but because that attempt failed, he had to figure out something else. He had to do something that would guarantee her death. He had to take control. The car fire was two weeks before Amber was murdered. The police said they would investigate, but when they went back to where the car had been on fire, the car was gone.

There was not even any ash. Everything had been cleaned up. Surely the investigating team thought to check the surveillance cameras. Amber's husband's next attempt on her life had to involve her in something that she could not get out of. His family didn't like that he married a white girl, but when you marry it is till death do you part. Amber's husband really should worry about when he meets his maker. I am fairly sure that conspiracy to commit murder is just as bad as murder in Gods eyes.

Our family believes that Amber's husband planned her death. We believe that her in laws have friends in high places. Amber was not what her husband expected. She fought back when he abused her. She wanted to divorce him and very well could have done that while he was in jail. Our family believes that Amber's husband and his family set up the killer to do a job for them.

That job was to get rid of Amber. Dispose of her body in New Mexico. Make it look like she was an addict who over dosed, but the killer they chose was too impatient for the drugs he gave her to take hold. Maybe Mr. Pearce got back to fast and that made the killer impatient. Maybe he thought he was about to get caught. Any way you look at it, Amber would have died that night.

I bet the killer was told not to worry about the mother-in-law getting ahold of Amber's body to look for evidence. I did call the New Mexico coroner's office, and the mortuary where my daughter's body was. I did try to get Amber's body home to Nebraska. I would have paid for a second autopsy. Of course, this is all just a bunch of theories. Or, is it all just theories?

The killer broke into Mr. Pearce's business. He stole guns. He took the guns to Amber to have her sell them. Why would he do that? Why would he take the guns to Amber? He would do that because someone told him to. Amber's husband was mad because he got caught in the stolen pickup. He blamed Amber. Amber's husband knew the story about her father. He knew that she wanted more than anything to find out more about her father. There wasn't anything more to find out about her father that I had not told her. Amber's husbands' mother could have got that information from her son, or even Amber herself.

The Investigators were told that Amber knew her killer because her killer knew her dad, and that her dad left him with a bunch of money for her. That was all just a lie to throw off the investigation. I asked the investigator to look into her killers' jail account to see if anyone was putting money on his books. I never heard anything back about that. Basically, since the husbands plan failed with the car lock rigging, he had to try again. When he tried again, he needed to make sure Amber died.

There has to be some kind of paper trail to prove that, but then again, the investigation is finished and sentences have been carried out. Amber's mother-in-law is also no longer with us. Amber's eldest daughter tried to find her mother's settlements, but had no luck. I'm sure the police either helped Amber's husband hide it or they stopped him from getting it.

Neither scenario would surprise me. After Amber's death that was the first thing her husband mentioned. How I should not worry, he would use Amber's settlement money to take care of Amber's children. I asked the police to stop her settlements if they could. Whatever they did, I didn't want Amber's husband to involved in my grandchildren's lives at all.

I will continue to say, Amber's husband and his family wanted Amber gone. I believe they wanted to train her children, especially her son who was *looking* for a father figure who would show him how to be a man. Amber's husband was not a man. The bad stuff he did, the crooked life he led, did not make him a man at all. Amber's husband took her son many places with him. Even to drug deals. He taught Amber's son how to shoot a gun.

They were going to take Amber's youngest daughter to her step great grandmother to hide her from me, but I showed up unexpectedly with papers signed by a Pueblo Judge. Both of my granddaughters can attest to that information. I foiled their plans for Amber's children!

I am so glad I was able to get my grandchildren home to safety. None of them miss or want that life ever again.

Because there was no trial no one was allowed to witness or testify anything. Everything in this book gives reason as to why there should have been a trial. There should never be circumstances for murder, unless it is self-defense! Amber did not get justice. Amber's husband should be sitting in a jail cell forever instead of running around trying to teach children how to be bad. If the world continues to allow criminals light sentence's, the world will pay. What are we teaching our children?

I originally thought Amber's old gang life caught up with her. There might still be some truth to that. I told the police my thoughts of conspiracy to kill Amber. I was wrong. I was full of grief. I tried to figure out something I had never experienced before. It wasn't the bad guys that lured her in with promises of a life of everything she wanted that killed her. It was her husband and his family.

Amber wasn't perfect but, she was my daughter, and I will say this one last time. It doesn't matter what she did, said, how she acted. Amber was my child and I loved her so very much. Amber did not deserve to die! For some reason the public seems to think that our daughter leaving her children with us should make us love her less or something. That's not how life works. The public seems to believe that when things go wrong, you're supposed to go hide in a hole. That's not how things work either.

Almost two years later I am still trying to work through the wrinkles of what happened to Amber. There are several certainties in Amber's death. Her husband was angry with her over getting arrested. His family did not like Amber. She didn't belong in his family, and they openly voice that.

Her husband set up her car to burn with her in it. Why else would he be so angry with her for checking up on the car. The man who worked on the car was to change a tire. Why was the hood open? Why was that man so surprised when Amber came back very much alive? Where did the burnt car go? Who cleaned up where the car had sat and burned?

Why did the man that killed Amber choose to take guns that he stole from Mr. Pearce to Amber? Why did the police focus on an obvious made-up story of the killer and Amber's dad being best friends? The investigator asked me about Amber's dad. I told her he died in 1994. Amber's dad actually died in 1992. It isn't likely at all that the killer knew Ambers biological father. If the man that killed Amber knew her dad, they both would have been children. Not grown men who met in prison in California. Are the investigators in Pueblo that lazy, or did they just not care?

CHAPTER SEVEN
The Media

The media reports inaccurate, incomplete stories all the time. The first news report I saw called Amber the Slain Woman. So disrespectful to Amber! So disrespectful to our family. They could have said Police Identify woman found near Pecos. Why be so disrespectful of Amber? Why did they label her like that? The second thing was, Amber wasn't a Deck anymore. Amber had an 8-year-old daughter who got to see this. She had an 11-year-old son who got to see this. She had friends who saw this. The media should not have rights over the victim's family! They did not have the right be so cruel.

The actual articles can be found on the internet by typing in a search for, "Amber Ann Deck". I am not pointing the finger at any one media source. I am complaining about all of them who reported Amber's death. These article sections are used only to point out actual facts! This is a short chapter because what I have to say did not take a complete chapter. I also changed the first highlighted statement.

> Amber Ann Deck, was not reported missing at all. So, that would be false reporting. *Amber Willhite was reported missing in Pueblo on May 22 prior to Pueblo police learning her body had been discovered the previous day.* **This highlighted sentence is completely false! Amber Winkenwerder / Willhite was first reported missing by her eldest daughter on the 17th of May! She called the police department daily to ask about her mother. Amber's husband conveniently reported her missing after it was to late to do anything for her. Her husband reported her missing as Amber**

Willhite!

The killers defense team argued that the majority of the evidence presented in court was hearsay and did not fit the state's charge of first-degree murder. **But we were repeatedly told that there was enough evidence!**

Law enforcement looked into a May 18 report of a burning vehicle outside of the Quality Inn on the north side. **The burning vehicle was because of her husband, but the investigator kept insisting that he had nothing to do with Amber's death! Lean on the guy that was told to rig her car! I bet he will turn on the whoever told him to rig her car. That car did not disappear into thin air. It is somewhere! Refer to Chapter Six!**

surveillance footage from the hotel, **Wouldn't the surveillance footage show who cleaned up the burnt car mess?**

Based on interviews with Pearce **Refer to Mr. Pearce's statements to me! Statements via jail mail.**

Then there is New Mexican's Against Gun Violence. When are people going to understand it's not guns that kill people? It wasn't a gun that pulled its own trigger. A person pulled the trigger on a gun that killed my daughter. You can take the guns away from the bad guys, but they will get more guns! Get rid of the bad guys! Wait, getting rid of the bad guys doesn't work either, because for every bad guy there are 50 more bad guys just like the one you got rid of. How about make those bad guys pay for their crimes!

Give them automatic life in prison for taking a life with those guns of theirs. Stop pandering to the whining lawyers and criminals. Criminals are getting worse because they get a slap on the hand. Television, a form of media, feeds into the criminal activity by creating shows that make them look like somebody's. That's dehumanizing victims.

Do away with criminal idolization! They might have been good people at some point in their life. Since these guys like guns so much put them in the front line in a war. Let's see how well they fare there. If they come back in one piece excuse their crime. If they don't, well, we just lost a criminal. You know kind of like the police looked at Amber as a criminal, and she was the victim!

The media screams fake news all the time. Yet they are faking the news. They leave out important details. It's Amber's turn to clear the air. Her name is Amber Winkenwerder – Willhite. The Media has been repeatedly told this. The media continued all the way through the investigation, and sentencing to print Amber Deck. Since they continue well after they were told Amber's actual name at the time of her death was Amber Ann Willhite.

Newsbreak Pueblo; published a very misleading article where they specifically misquoted me. They left out most of what I said in court. Newsbreak was also misleading in publishing what my granddaughter said. They did not skip a beat where Mr. Pearce was concerned. Misleading!!! Again, they published their articles about Amber Deck. Repeatedly using Deck in reference. Newsbreak left out that I mentioned that it was almost Amber's 35th birthday. I told the court that it would be nice if Amber could get justice by her birthday. If the news is going to report they should have reported everything.

The media gets by with too much these days. Putting the Slain Woman label on Amber was horrible for her children to see. I would like to see a media public apology over that. Straight out the gate they dehumanized Amber. They kept up their distrustful ways by reporting her as a Deck clear through all of the court appearances. The media showed clear disregard to Amber's family by not reporting her name correctly. They could have cleared that up by saying her name was reported incorrectly at the time of discovery, but they chose to ignore Amber's family.

All the media that reported Amber's death, whether they piggy backed off another media source or not, needs to publish a public apology to Amber's family for being distrustful, inconsiderate, dehumanizing to Amber, and providing misleading information to the public. My daughter wasn't perfect, but she did not deserve such blatant disregard to her as a person. They also need to remove every article they wrote about Amber. I doubt that they will, but eventually I will make them remove it all. I took two years to research and write this book; I don't want to continue seeing all of this.

The Chieftain also reported what I said in court incorrectly. They omitted a lot of what I, and my granddaughter said. Omitting is misleading, as is publishing incorrectly. The only thing Amber did wrong was she got herself involved with the wrong people. She did not shoot herself. She did not place her dead body into a tote. No matter how heartfelt Mr. Pearce's statement to me or otherwise, Amber deserved some damn respect. She is the one who was shot dead.

She was the victim, and so was her family! The Police, investigating team, DA's office, Victim Services, and the Judge herself showed Amber little to no respect. They showed our family the same disrespect. The courts concern should have been protecting the victim and her family. Getting justice for Amber instead of protecting the rights of the person who killed her should have been the number one priority. That was not the case. Very sad display of the justice system in Pueblo, Colorado. They should be ashamed of themselves!

CHAPTER EIGHT
Don't Make Your Loved Ones Go Through This!

Most of us know about the dangers of drugs. Apparently, some of us have not received the dangers of drugs memo. Amber got that memo. I drilled the say no to drugs into my children's heads. I do not do drugs, and I do not tolerate doing drugs. I suppose that is why I have been accused of abandoning Amber. Why did I order Amber's toxicology report? I ordered it because I wanted to see if she was high when she died. The following is a list of the drugs that were evident in Amber's blood. It appears, Amber might have known she had been shot, but thankfully, probably did not suffer in her death.

Postmortem, Basic, Blood (Forensic) – Heart Blood

Amphetamines 20 ng/mL

Barbiturates   0.040 mcg/mL

Benzodiazepine 100 ng/mL

Buprenorphine/Metabolite 0.50 ng/mL

Cannabinoids   10 ng/mL

Cocaine / Metabolites   20 ng/mL

Fentanyl / Acetyl Fentanyl 0.50 ng/mL

Methadone / Metabolite 25 ng/mL

Methamphetamine / MDMA   20 ng/mL

Opiates 20 ng/mL

Oxycodone / Oxymorphone   10 ng/mL

Phencyclidine 10ng/mL

Positive Findings:			
Compound	Result	Units	Matrix Source
Ethanol	27	mg/dL	001 - Heart Blood
Blood Alcohol Concentration (BAC)	0.027	g/100 mL	001 - Heart Blood
Amphetamine	32	ng/mL	001 - Heart Blood
Methamphetamine	170	ng/mL	001 - Heart Blood

It is clear that Amber had drugs in her blood when she died. How these drugs got in her is unknown. It is not clear if Amber had help putting the drugs into her system. Amber did have defensive wounds on her fingers. Amber's hands were covered with brown bags.

The New Mexico Coroners office findings validate Mr. Pearce's claims that Amber's killer kicked her in the face before he shot her twice in her chest.

Don't make your loved one have to look up the affects of what you took! Below are the various definitions for each drug in Amber's system. I have cited each search I did during my quest of understanding my daughters last day alive. Mr. Pearce's claims of Amber being quite verbal are also validated by the coroners' report.

Amphetamines

Is a synthetic, addictive, mood-altering drug, used illegally as a stimulant and legally as a prescription drug to treat children with ADD and adults with narcolepsy.

"The amphetamine put him on a high for an hour"

Barbiturates

Class of drugs

Description

Barbiturates are a class of depressant drugs that are chemically derived from barbituric acid. They are effective when used medically as anxiolytics, hypnotics, and anticonvulsants, but have physical and psychological addiction potential as well as overdose potential among other possible adverse effects. Wikipedia

Benzodiazepine

What are Benzodiazepines? Benzodiazepines are depressants that produce sedation and hypnosis, relieve anxiety and muscle spasms, and reduce seizures. The most common benzodiazepines are the prescription drugs Valium®, Xanax®, Halcion®, Ativan®, and Klonopin®. Dea.gov

Buprenorphine

Wikipedia

https://en.wikipedia.org › wiki › Buprenorphine

*Buprenorphine is metabolized **by the liver, via CYP3A4** (also CYP2C8 seems to be involved) isozymes of the cytochrome P450 enzyme system, ...*

Metabolism: Liver (CYP3A4, CYP2C8) Elimination half-life: 37 hours

Cannabinoids

What are cannabinoids? The word cannabinoid refers to every chemical substance, regardless of structure or origin, that joins the cannabinoid receptors of the body and brain and that have similar effects to those produced by the Cannabis Sativa plant.

Cocaine / Metabolites

***Benzoylecgonine** is the main metabolite of cocaine, formed by the liver and excreted in the urine. It is the compound tested for in most cocaine urine drug screens and in wastewater screenings for cocaine use.*

Wikipedia

Fentanyl / Acetyl Fentanyl

Acetyl fentanyl

Drug

Description

Acetyl fentanyl is an opioid analgesic drug that is an analog of fentanyl. Studies have estimated acetyl fentanyl to be fifteen times more potent than morphine, which would mean that despite being somewhat weaker than fentanyl, it is nevertheless still several times stronger than pure heroin. Wikipedia

Methadone / Metabolite

Methadone Metabolite (EDDP), Urine, Qualitative Screen

University of Michigan

https://mlabs.umich.edu › tests › methadone-metabolite...

This test is for the qualitative detection of **methadone metabolite** (2-ethylene-1,5-dimethyl-3,3-diphenylpyrrolidine or EDDP) in urine at a cutoff concentration

Methamphetamine / MDMA

Drug Fact Sheet: Ecstasy/MDMA

DEA.gov

https://www.dea.gov › Ecstasy-MDMA-2020_0

WHAT IS ECSTASY/**MDMA**? **MDMA** acts as both a stimulant and psychedelic, producing an energizing effect, distortions in time and perception, and enhance

Opiates

Opioid

Medication

Description

Opioids are substances that act on opioid receptors to produce morphine-like effects. Medically they are primarily used for pain relief, including anesthesia. Other medical uses include suppression of diarrhea, replacement therapy for opioid use disorder, reversing opioid overdose, and suppressing cough. Wikipedia

Use: Pain relief **Mode of action:** Opioid receptor

Oxycodone / Oxymorphone

Clinical Information

Oxymorphone is metabolized in the liver to noroxymorphone and excreted via the kidney primarily as the glucuronide conjugates. Oxymorphone is also a metabolite of oxycodone and, therefore, the presence of oxymorphone *could also indicate exposure to oxycodone. Testcatalog.org*

Phencyclidine

Phencyclidine, 1-(1-phenylcyclohexyl) piperidine, is a white crystalline powder, which is readily soluble in water or alcohol. PCP is classified as a hallucinogen. PCP is a "dissociative" drug; it induces distortion of sight and sound and produces feelings of detachment.

PHENCYCLIDINE - DEA Diversion

I did not do all this research because I wanted to write Amber's story. I researched the New Mexico Coroners' report so that I could understand what my daughter went through in her final moments. I have boxes of research because of Amber's death. I examined her autopsy over and over. The book plan came later after our family discussed the benefits to others of writing Amber's story. Our hopes are that we can help other families understand that the drugs changed how their person thought. How they felt is not how you remember them.

Amber was not herself. Her brain lived in a fantasy world where everything around her only made sense to her and others doing the same drugs. She could not relate to the real world any longer. The only thing that she lived was the constant disoriented life that the drug feeling gave to her. The feeling that she was invincible. The fake power that she craved. She controlled her life in such a way that I do not understand. I can not understand how a drug induced existence can feel good at all. I can imagine that other families struggle understanding this same thing.

The way people look at the drug problem needs work. We need to stop blaming the people who are addicted and deal with the drug problem. Trafficker's deliver the drugs from state to state. Doctors prescribe these same drugs to people. Big pharma pushes their drugs to those doctors that are giving their patients these drugs. How do people not see that their own doctors are getting them addicted to the very drugs that are being trafficked. It is a never-ending cycle, until people do something about it. Maybe natures way is the best way. I prefer herbal remedies to any drug that can turn me into an addict.

CHAPTER NINE
Two Years Gone

It has been two years since our family lost Amber. The first year is almost a complete blur. We brought the kids home. We put them back in school. The first school year Amber's son could not even handle being around people. He was scared, angry, hurt, confused, and he refused counseling. I thought, because my grandson was telling me, that he was having Native American brown boy issues, that teachers at the school were focusing on him in a negative racial way. I set him up to go to school in Lexington where almost all the kids are Hispanic, brown children.

I thought he would fit in better. I drove him 24 miles, one way, every day. That did not work. I attempted homeschooling my grandson to help him gain his confidence back. That did not work. What helped Amber's son was his big sister coming home. Somewhere along the way in a 7-month time frame, my grandson lost a piece of who he used to be. He came home to me a young man. The little boy I knew was no more.

Amber's children are the true victims in this story. Amber's eldest daughter received most of the mistreatment because she is Amber's eldest.

At 18 years old she had to deal with the most traumatizing parts of her mothers' death. Amber's daughter had to go to the police station and listen to them talk about the body of a woman they found in New Mexico. They did not tell her that the body they found was her mother. So, the police who are supposed to serve and protect made an 18-year-old sit there wondering what her mother did.

They made her sit there for hours, asking her questions about her mother. When they finally told her the body, they found was Amber's she got overwhelmed. Amber's mother-in-law went with her and sat there letting them toy with her. The mother-in-law did not try to comfort her. Several of the investigators laughed at her. The Sargant even laughed at her. You might be thinking, no that can't be. Investigators are trained to be professional. Oh, but it happened, and it makes me incredibly angry.

After the police told Amber's eldest daughter that the body, they found was her mother, she fell apart. It could not be true. She asked them if they were sure, it was her mother. The New Mexico investigator told her, he was sure. They identified her by her finger prints through the FBI. That is how they learned that at one time Amber had the Deck surname.

That is why the media started publishing reports about Amber Ann Deck. That is why it is so disrespectful that they continued to refer to her as Deck. She had not been a Deck for many, many years. After interviewing Amber's daughter and confirming that Amber was a Willhite, the respectful thing to do would be to correct her name to her current married name. That was not important enough to them, though.

Amber's husband was in jail the entire investigating process, and most of the court process. Amber's daughter wanted to do right by her mother, but was not allowed to. I think she wanted her mother sent home to Nebraska. I wanted that too. I wanted to have my daughter's body looked at by a Nebraska mortuary, but my son-in-law had different plans. He put his mother in charge of setting my daughter up to be cremated.

We believe he did that to destroy the evidence Amber still had in her body. Amber's daughter was not allowed to be involved in anything that had to do with her mother, or her mother's body. That frustrated her to no end. When she wanted to see the crime scene photos, she was told by her step grandmother that the photos would be looked at by a professional to see if she could manage them.

The step grandmother gave the image CD to her daughter who is not a professional. She told her mother that Amber's daughter would not be able to handle the images, and she deleted the images and destroyed the CD. She had no right to make decisions about what Amber's daughter could or could not handle. She was not a professional at all. She just did not want her see the images.

Amber's daughter was hospitalized shortly after her mother's death. Her brother saw it on Tic Tok and told me about it. I asked her about her illness when she came home to me. Her step grandmother cooked food for everyone except herself. Why wouldn't she eat the food she made? Her own daughter wouldn't eat the food her mother made, and would make excuses as to why she wouldn't eat the food her mother made.

I find that extremely weird because I love my cooking and eat what I make. Not only that, but Amber's daughter has not been hospitalized since she returned home. She eats the food I cook every day. Interesting!

The in-laws who claimed to be so supportive were not supportive at all. They were mentally abusive, controlling, and self-serving. My grandchildren were told to lie to the school about their mothers' death, but there was only one day of school left. My youngest granddaughter who is the most like her mother, was told she was going to be in trouble for telling the truth!

What on earth for? The principle himself said they would have been excused from school because they should not have been there. Their mother died, and that was extremely hard on the kids. So, I ask you, what was wrong with those people? How could they be so cruel to children who just lost their mother in the worse way possible?

Let's add topping to this shameful cake. Right after Amber's killer was sentenced, and because there was no trial, Amber's mother-in-law kicked the eldest daughter out of her house. Since there wasn't a trial, they no longer needed her.

Had there been a trial she would have had to be in court as a witness. They needed to manipulate her if a trial happened. I had Amber's other children by that time. I doubt that Amber's eldest daughter would go against what her siblings were saying. This is proof that the in laws were a part of Amber's murder. Why would they want her dead?

I think what the in-laws saw were 3 distraught children whose pain could be used to benefit their cause.

Pain is a powerful tool. They could use that pain to harden those children thus making them into gang members.

While all that was going on, Amber's youngest had her own issues. She wanted what her brother was getting. She wanted special treatment. Big brother wasn't getting special treatment, but she thought he was. So, she colored along the elbow veins, to make it look like someone had stomped on her arm so hard that they bruised her veins. I know, it sounds crazy. She then told me how bad her elbow hurt, and even blamed a classmate of doing that to her.

We took her to the doctor, and her grandpa went in with her. When he came out the look on his face was beyond annoyed. I knew, and he had the evidence. I tried using alcohol to see if she had colored on her veins, but it didn't come off. The doctor used medical grade alcohol on a cotton ball, and grandpa was holding the green inked cotton ball in his fingers. He gruffly told the youngest of Amber's children to tell me what she did. She told me, and she did not like that she had to tell me, because I earlier took her for ice-cream because I felt bad for her.

I did transfer her to Lexington schools, even though I explained to her that her brother was not getting special treatment, and she was not going to get on well at the schools in Lexington. She is a very white only 39% Mexican girl. Amber's youngest did not like the choice she made, but I made her stick with it.

Every day I explained to her that she was going to go to school, even though she very much wanted me to transfer her back to her old school, it was too late to put her back in her old school. The last day of school Amber's youngest was so happy, but she asked me if she had to go back the next year. I told her she made it through, she saw what her choice caused her, and she would go to her old school the next year.

Summer came and went too fast. Amber's son and his friend took turns staying at each other's houses. Big sister went to her old friend's house. I spent the entire summer with Amber's youngest. It was a rough summer, but we made it through. We did not do anything special. We did take the kids to various fairs in the area including the State fair. Amber's youngest daughter's 10th birthday came and went. We took her to spend a day at the pool, with her sister, her grandpa, and me. Her brother was visiting his friend. We took her out to eat as well.

Amber's son's birthday marks the beginning of the new school year. He did not want a day with his sister's. Grandpa and I took him go carting with his best friend. We ordered pizza for him, because that is what he wanted, and we had his birthday celebration the weekend before his birthday, because of school starting. His dad told him he was going to do a birthday celebration for him, but that did not happen, even though his dad celebrated Amber's youngest daughters' birthday with her. He could not manage to find the time to celebrate his son's birthday.

His dad did help pay for a new dirt bike for his son's special day. Amber's son felt let down once again.

In an attempt to show our grandson how special he is, we allowed him a second birthday dinner of pizza since his dad made him feel so horrible. This is proof of what drugs do the people you care about. In all fairness Amber's youngest son did get to go to Lincoln with his new step mom to visit his dad. They took him to a trampoline place and he had a blast with his dad. The thing with Amber's youngest son's dad, is that he has never really been there for his son. He doesn't know him, he has tried, somewhat. I do hope that some day he can cut the drug ties that bind him so he can get to know his son before it's too late.

September is a rough month for me. My adopted mother died the day before my birthday, my biological father died 2 days before my birthday, and now Amber wasn't with us anymore. It was also the first year without Amber so my emotions were amplified. Nothing special happened aside from my normal steak, potatoes, salad, and popcorn shrimp birthday meal. I did have a pretty good day considering it's not the best of months.

October 1st is my big brothers' birthday, just had to mention that because it's special to him and me. While we are on the subject of my big brother. I would like to point out how supportive he truly is.

He was there for me when the police told me that we <u>might</u> have to go into witness protection because they did not know who killed Amber, and they did not know how much if any danger the children were in. When the killer was arrested the danger to the children was gone.

October is the month our little booligans look forward to almost as much as the 4th of July, Christmas, and their birthdays. They very much enjoy and get into the Halloween spirit. These kids love to dress up scary. As much as they love dressing up scary, they love getting free candy, money, and sodas even more. They also went to the haunted house this year. It's in Holdrege, and from what I hear, it's the best haunted house! It is so fun to have these kids with us. They are so adventurous, and they get so excited that they make me excited. I don't get excited much anymore. Amber's youngest did not go to the haunted house because it was just a bit too scary for her.

November as everyone knows is the Thanksgiving time of the year. We are thankful, but we did not celebrate the traditional Thanksgiving because we have a Native American in our life. It's disrespectful to make him celebrate something that he knows wronged his people. We feasted that's for sure. We spent time together; we all had a great time.

December brings weeks off school, and what child doesn't like that. The first year brought our family a lot of pain. Money was strapped because we had just paid lawyer fees, and court ordered DNA fees because the judge working our custody case insisted for everyone's sake to have Amber's youngest DNA tested again the son's father. It was the Native American thing. Still, we had to pay for it at the worse time of the year.

The BIA insisted we eliminate Amber's youngest daughter from having Native American claims of any sort.

January in my world brings a lot of birthdays. My eldest daughter, my youngest son, and Amber. It was the first time we celebrated

Amber's 1st heavenly birthday. We had black cows for her birthday, and red velvet cake. Her favorite special things. Her meal was steak, baked potatoes, and salad. Almost the same as my favorite meal so, I didn't mind. It was delicious. We lit a candle for her for the entire day. What's a black cow? Vanilla ice cream with Pepsi poured over. Yummm!

February brought us Amber's killers sentencing date. We all got on Webex to see that horrible person. There wasn't much to see, and court did not last long. I was at all but one Webex court sessions. The only one I missed was the first one, and that was because I did not know how to work the Webex yet. The session I missed brought a slew of bad remarks from our in-laws.

If they were me, they would have done everything in their power to be at ever court date. Yet they only went to the first court date. I am pretty sure they stopped coming because they received news that the DA's office talked me into accepting their plea deal. Amber's killer jumped on the plea deal. He confessed to shooting Amber twice in her chest.

Before we knew it the first anniversary of Amber's murder was on us. I felt like nothing was ever going to get better. Amber's youngest was constantly getting into trouble at school. Her son was struggling with even wanting to go to school.

Then summer came again. We repeated the Nebraska fairs, because the kids really enjoyed going to them and it took their minds off their lives being so screwy. Birthdays came and went. The second year wasn't as hard as the first year, but it was still hard. We sold our retirement house. That made things a bit easier.

Things started getting less and less stressful. Amber's eldest daughter and I talked through a lot of things. She has been through so much more because she was the eldest. The second year Thanksgiving and Christmas were financially better, as we no longer had lawyer fees to deal with. The kids had a better holiday with one exception. The father of Amber's son showed up high. No one wanted a repeat of drug induced holidays. He was told if you are going to come around high don't bother coming around. So, he has stayed away. Sad really.

January came around and Sean Pearce had his sentencing. Refer to Mr. Pearce's' Discovery statement. We hoped if we could get the judge to go to trial that his trial would provoke a retrial for Amber's killer, but Mr. Pearce had a plea deal as well. He too accepted his plea deal, and he did speak about his ordeal. I could feel Amber during his speech to our family. After court I felt empty. I felt like Amber wasn't ever going to get justice. All our chances to help her get justice were over. Then Amber's voice popped into my head. "You did what you could do momma. Leave the rest to me."

All my January birthdays came around where we sent our eldest daughter birthday money. My son had his birthday meal. Amber had her birthday meal. Then is when I decided to get to work on her book.

I decided it was time to show the world what drugs do to families. I started her book long before then, but at that time it was just therapeutic. I talked to Amber's children and asked them if they wanted me to write their mother's story. They did want it. Amber's children wanted me to write her story to help the children of other addicts. They felt alone through everything they went through. They felt like no one understood them, or what they have been through. I imagine a lot of children can relate to how my grandchildren feel.

After Amber married her last husband, she changed a lot. That is why we think as we do. He and his family tried to break that free spirit of hers, but they couldn't break Amber. With those kinds of people, if you can't break her get rid of her. They tried once and it failed. She kicked her way out of a burning car! It took a bullet to her heart to stop Amber. Even then they did not stop her. They set her spirit free!

CHAPTER TEN
In Honor of Our Amber

I had 3 sons' before I had my eldest daughter. I wanted a little girl more than anything. Then I met Amber's father. Our relationship wasn't a serious one. I didn't think it was. He did though. After I took off home to Nebraska in the middle of the night with 3 boys, he literally went through trash to find my phone bill and called my adopted parents. I suppose, I thought that since he went through so much trouble to be with me, I might as well give him a chance.

I allowed him to stay on one condition. He needed to stop drinking. I worked, he stayed with the kids. He saved me a ton on babysitting money. It was really nice to come home from work to supper on the stove or sometimes the table. He was alright to talk to. Nice to look at. My boys loved playing with him. I got used to Amber's dad helping out and being there for me.

He made coming home nicer. We decided with baby number 4 coming soon to get a bigger place. We lived in a trailer park, because that is what I could afford on my waitress wages. Fortunately for us someone had recently moved out of a bigger trailer. I spoke to the manager and we began moving the next day. All our moving put me into labor. I noticed that my boys needed milk for breakfast so I sent Amber's dad out to get milk.

I continued putting things away. I pulled boxes across the floor to get things where I wanted them without lifting them. Then it happened! My water broke.

Amber's dad was not back with the milk. It was after 1 A.M. when I saw the headlight shine on the front door. I angrily told him to give me the keys, take care of the boys, and we would discuss where he had been after I had my baby. I drove myself to the hospital. I walked myself through the emergency room doors, the lady behind the desk took one look at me and grabbed a wheel chair. In the morning I called my friend to check on everything at my house. Apparently, Amber's dad was doing a great job with the boys. He even walked over to the hospital while the boys were in school to get the car.

I forgave him when I got home and saw how nice everything looked at home. A year and a few days after my first baby girl graced my world, baby Amber came. Amber's dad did the exact same thing during Amber's birth. He got drunk, then tried to make up. We broke up after Amber was born. He tried to steal her from the daycare. The daycare saw him attack me and called the police. When the police pulled up Amber's dad had me bent backwards over the handrailing. The Officer jumped the rail and took Amber's dad to the ground. I went inside the daycare.

By the time I got the kids ready the Officer was gone and so was Amber's dad. I received a call from a social worker a few weeks later. Amber's dad wanted one visit before he left to go back to California. I agreed, but parked where I could see his motel room. He spent 30 minutes with Amber. She was only a couple of weeks old.

Amber's dad overdosed in 1992. We were not close, and I did not speak to him after I picked up Amber that last day. From 1988 to 1992 Amber's dad never contacted us again.

My little girls were so adorable. They were so smart, and talented. I did spend a lot of time with Amber because Amber was my baby. When I got off work, I picked up Amber first then went to get her sister and brothers. All my children had their moments, but generally they were thick as thieves when it came to protecting each other. Amber was the first in her kindergarten class to know all her colors, her numbers to 100 and her ABC's. My second to the oldest son loved taking Amber on lawn mowing jobs because she always helped him get special treats after most jobs.

As a little girl Amber was too friendly. I always had to remind her not to talk to strangers. *They aren't stranger's mommy. They are friends.* Amber was a straight A student like her sister. Her sister was a great role model. As a matter of fact, I think that Amber was my instigator and her sister was very much my calm girl.

Amber made older friends. Like the lady across the corner from where we lived when she was about 10. I don't know how she met her. I think she just went up to the lady's door and asked her if she could help her by doing chores. She always asked me if she could go help the lady across the street. When she came back, she only had 50 cents, but she was ready to go get herself some candy.

Amber did not have problems making friends. She had a best friend who she loved dearly.

Those two would fight like cats and dogs one minute then be back in each other's good books the next minute. Amber was a good friend. She was caring and a trouble maker all wrapped in one. She was fun and she was a thrill seeker. Amber could keep a secret unless it was moms, she was keeping the secret for. She blabbered everything I told her to keep a secret. She also couldn't keep secrets at Christmas time. She got that from me. Amber was extremely loyal! It hurt her deeply when she gave loyalty but didn't receive it back.

I know, Amber's best friend will never forget the trip we took to California. Amber had to have her friend come along. We went to California because my youngest son and eldest daughter's grandmother was dying of cancer. She wanted to see all of her grandchildren one last time.

I told Amber it was alright for her friend to come along, as long as it was alright with her mother. Along the way we stopped at a motel. It was pretty late and very dark. Had I been alone I would have just stopped at a rest area to rest, but children get scared of noises. I checked 7 of us into a room. The motel matron looked at me like I was crazy, but she gave me my key, and pointed me to my room.

There was a lot of pent-up energy in those kids that night. They ran the halls; they tried not to be too noisy, but they were noisy and mischievous. They played at the hot tub until some guy showed up there and creeped the girls out. I don't remember my boys doing anything except watching television in the room. Those girls though, phew, they were so hyper. I received a call from the front desk.

I needed to get the kids calmed down and stop them from knocking on doors and running the halls or we would have to leave. I went to the door gathered up the girls and told them it was time to calm themselves down or we would have to leave. The girls apologized for running a muck and they did calm down. Giggles and snorts turned into sleepy yawns, and finally we were able to get some sleep.

The next morning, we went for breakfast, and my keys got locked in my van. My son had to crawl into one of the small windows to get the keys for me. That trip was the most fun I remember having with all my children, despite my son getting ill because he messed with something that stung him. I think all the kids had a lot of fun, and if I could do it all again, I definitely would.

As Amber grew up, she matured and began having her own ideas about how life was supposed to go. I suppose every child does that. She developed her likes and dislikes. She had favorite things to do. She picked up my love of gardening which made me extremely happy. She didn't have a green thumb though.

By holding onto the things, I showed her Amber was showing me that she still had those important things in her mind. In Pueblo at the first house, she lived in she tilled the front yard. She planted grass seed. She made flower beds and planted tulips. She called me to talk flowers. She sounded so happy then. Those moments told me she was holding on to her momma and the things her momma taught her.

Her favorite color was green. Her favorite food used to be similar to mine. She developed a love for Mexican food. I have no idea where that came from. I used to tease her about being part

Mexican. She teased me right back with *mom your racist*. Once, she asked me what I would do if She gave me part Mexican grandchildren. I told her that of course I would love them. They would be babies. Then she gave me part Mexican grandbabies to love. That was Amber. Always going against the grain.

She did what she wanted to do, when she wanted to do it. She forced acceptance in everything she did. She made her own rules, then changed them to suit her. She wanted everyone she met to like her, and she would get upset and take it personally if everyone didn't like her. Our Amber was a beautiful, complicated woman, who demanded acceptance everywhere she went. Her way was the right way, and she would work on you until you saw whatever her point was to be the right way. She was never wrong. You were. When proven wrong, she smiled and walked away.

Amber always stuck up for the underdog, children, abused women, animals, especially dogs. Every stray dog ended up being taken in and loved by Amber. She wanted normal, but always said there is no such thing as normal. Amber wanted to fix any wrongs she did, but thought that everything she did was wrong. Even her final day on earth she tried to fix what she thought she did wrong. It wasn't her wrong to make right. That wrong belonged to her murderer and whoever had him kill her.

As complicated as Amber was, she was our Amber! We didn't love many of the things she did or some of her choices, but we did love her. She was in no way going to win mother of the year awards, but she did love her children and her children loved the time they had with her. They miss her hugs. They miss her voice. I think they even miss arguing with her.

If I could speak to Amber one last time, I would tell her, and I have, that no one let her down more than she and I did. I am her mother. I protected her too much. I did not make her answer for her mistakes. Instead, I made excuses for the stupid things she did. I enabled her to go down the path she took.

I did not fight hard enough to keep her on the straight and narrow.

It was me that gave into Amber the most. I never wanted anything bad for her, but everything in her life went so crazy. I did not ever give up on her. I always felt when things were not as she said they were, but tried to convince her she was doing the right thing. She just needed to see the good things she did do.

It was wonderful that she protected those who needed protecting, but that was not her purpose in life. Protection is meant for the police, and she should have called them to protect those she saw being hurt by others. She should not have tried to take that on herself. It is good that she wanted to protect children, but she had children at home who needed her to protect them.

I am sure there are many things I don't know about my daughter. I do know enough. I know that she didn't want her life to end. I know when her life passed before her, she thought about her family. I know she was worried about us and how we would take her death.

We didn't take her death well. I wanted Amber's pain to end, but not like it did. I wanted my daughter back, but did not know how to get her back. I don't even know if it was possible to get her back, had she not been murdered.

Amber's struggles were a daily occurrence. It was not like she struggled some days and not other days. She was alone in her battle because she could not see her family was waiting for a turning point. Her children wanted to and tried to help her. I wanted to and tried to help her. Amber felt like she could do no right. I truly wish she could have seen all the right she did do. I wish she could see the acceptance her family had for her. She needed to see how much we all loved her.

Amber could not see the good in herself. A combination of the drugs she took and the people she hung around clouded her self judgement. The system consistently set her up for failure. Costing her more than she could make just trying to make ends meet. The men in her life continually degraded her self-dignity. After years of destructive behavior, one tends to believe they are no good.

Amber did fight hard for many years. Ultimately, and regrettably, Amber lost the fight with her demons. We believe, God called Amber home, because enough was enough. It is important for people to understand that it was not God that set Amber up in the situation where she was shot and killed. Amber chose to go with her killer. Neither God, nor Amber chose for her life to end the way it did. Amber's killer made the choice to shoot and kill Amber.

AFTERWORD

The loss of a parent is something most of us dread. When you are a child and you lose a parent in such a traumatic way, such as murder, it is devastating! Children don't understand why they didn't get to say goodbye. They don't understand why their parent was murdered. Children of murdered parents are forced to accept the loss of their parent with kind words. Well, I'm sorry for your loss does not help. I'm sorry for your loss does not answer children's questions. The children are forced to deal with something most of us never have to think about.

The purpose of this book was to help other families. Grief is difficult, but grief from murder is multiplied by other people not understanding the pain children and families go through because their loved one was murdered.

Therefore our family has discovered there is a need for us to start a foundation. It may take time, and that is alright, but 50% of the royalties from this book will be saved to begin, The Carol and Amber Foundation. Why 50%? Because Amber's children need to go to college. They need help to grow up. They still need help in understanding that their mother can never come back. Amber's death was not just some elaborate scheme. Her death was real! The effects that followed are real!

Spirit Bond Publishing along with Hugh Murphy (Author of,

Memories and Observations.) want to help those who are in need of Legal assistance, counseling, or a way to begin again. When I brought my grandchildren home they had one bag of clothes each. Clothes are expensive. That is what our foundation will do. It will help those forced to start over!

What can readers do? You can help us help other's by leaving a kind review. The purchase of this book helped! Sharing our story helps us get the word out. We don't want anyone to feel alone. Please, let's help each other, by bringing awareness. This is what Amber wants!

To leave a nice review